THE UNIVERSITY OF MICHIGAN
CENTER FOR CHINESE STUDIES

MICHIGAN PAPERS IN CHINESE STUDIES
NO. 34

THE MING DYNASTY
ITS ORIGINS AND EVOLVING INSTITUTIONS

by
Charles O. Hucker

Ann Arbor

Center for Chinese Studies
The University of Michigan

1978

*Open access edition funded by the National Endowment for the Humanities/
Andrew W. Mellon Foundation Humanities Open Book Program.*

Published by
Center for Chinese Studies
The University of Michigan

Library of Congress Cataloging in Publication Data

Hucker, Charles O.
    The Ming dynasty, its origins and evolving institutions.

    (Michigan papers in Chinese studies; no. 34)
    Includes bibliographical references.
    1. China--History--Ming dynasty, 1368-1644. I. Title.
II. Series.
DS753.H829   951'.026   78-17354
ISBN 0-89264-034-0

Printed and bound by CPI Group (UK) Ltd, Croydon, CR0 4YY

ISBN 978-0-89264-034-8 (hardcover)
ISBN 978-0-472-03812-1 (paper)
ISBN 978-0-472-12758-0 (ebook)
ISBN 978-0-472-90153-1 (open access)

CONTENTS

PREFACE

This long essay was written in 1970 to fit into an outline of what was then planned to be Volume IV of The Cambridge History of China, edited by Professors Denis Twitchett and John K. Fairbank. Unfortunately, publication of all portions of the history has been long postponed, and it appears that the Ming volume (or volumes) may not be available for several more years. Moreover, plans have been so altered that my contribution is not likely to fit the new Ming outline without substantial rearrangement and revision. I am nevertheless persuaded that the original effort has sufficient validity and integrity to deserve independent preservation. It is therefore issued belatedly in this series. The Center for Chinese Studies and I are grateful to the Syndics of the Cambridge University Press for allowing it to be so issued without relinquishing their proprietary rights.

Guidelines for contributors to the Cambridge History account for some characteristics of the presentation. It is offered in the form of an essay rather than a research monograph; it is not technical in style, and it is annotated only minimally. It strives for factual accuracy and clarity without unreasonable oversimplification, but it does not shrink from distinctively personal interpretations and judgments.

I am surprised and gratified that the passage of seven years, in which the volume of scholarly work on Ming China has grown enormously, has not significantly altered my 1970 interpretations and judgments. For useful criticisms of the original draft I am deeply indebted to many colleagues in the Ming studies field, most notably Professors F. W. Mote, John Dardess, Lo Jung-pang, L. Carrington Goodrich, and Ray Huang. I have perhaps not benefitted fully from all their suggestions, but I have attempted to rectify all factual errors that they have called to my attention. Otherwise, the essay is presented substantially in its 1970 form. For whatever errors may remain, and for all matters of organization and interpretation, I accept full responsibility.

Rather than attempt to update what was always meager annotation, I offer the Notes in their original form. I cannot fail to point out, however, that almost every section of this work can now be examined from a biographical point of view in the monumental Dictionary of Ming Biography, edited by L. Carrington Goodrich (2 volumes; New York: Columbia University Press, 1976). Also, some of the unpublished manuscripts cited in the Notes are now available, in some cases revised, in published form: for example, Romeyn Taylor's Basic Annals of Ming T'ai-tsu (San Francisco: Chinese Materials Center, 1975) and Edward L. Farmer's Early Ming Government: The Evolution of Dual Capitals (Cambridge: Harvard University Press, 1976).

Charles O. Hucker
Ann Arbor, Michigan
August 1977

I. Introduction

In the latter half of the fourteenth century, when at the opposite end of the Eurasian continent the stage was not yet set for the emergence of modern nation-states, the Chinese drove out their Mongol overlords, inaugurated a new native dynasty called Ming (1368-1644), and reasserted mastery of their national destiny. It was a dramatic era of change, the full significance of which can only be perceived retrospectively.

The conquest by the Mongols and their century-long military occupation had been an unprecedented shock for the Chinese, despite their long experience of fighting off or, alternatively, accommodating northern invaders. Never before had all Chinese been subjugated by aliens, and never before had leadership roles in China been so thoroughly preempted by outsiders as was the case with the Mongols and their non-Chinese hangers-on. The natural leaders of China's traditional society, the educated landowners, had been partly killed off in the conquest. Survivors and would-be successors had been either drawn into collaboration with the conquerors for profit or from confused conceptions of loyalty, or driven into apolitical eremitism and dilettantism. In either case, their potentiality as leaders of rebellion withered. The consequence was that China's recovery, when it came, was equally unprecedented, in that it was led, as it were by default, by men of the lowest social classes devoid of roots in the traditional high culture. This circumstance lent to the recovery process much of its drama and significance. It is noteworthy that China's recovery was also sudden and decisive and that it brought into being a new-style state system that would endure into the twentieth century and shape the style of China's eventual efforts to cope with modernization in the dynamically evolving Western mode.

Small-scale popular uprisings had been endemic throughout the Mongols' Yüan dynasty (1260-1368), but these were phenomena that were common in all periods of China's imperial history, part of the danger-filled and violence-prone normalcy that characterized the

1

traditional Chinese society and polity. It was not until 1351 that the
Mongols' confident grip on China began to slip ominously. Then, disin-
tegration of the empire came swiftly. By 1358 rebels controlled the
whole Yangtze River, from modern Szechwan province in the west to
the sea in the east, as well as the whole east coast from Shantung province in the north to Fukien province in the south; and North China rebels
had even raided and burned the Mongols' summer capital, Shang-tu in
modern Chahar province (the fabled Xanadu), far beyond the Great Wall.
For another decade rebels in central China struggled among themselves
for supremacy while the Yüan government at modern Peking stood by
distractedly. When issues were resolved in the south and a consolidated
revolutionary movement turned its forces northward in 1368, Mongol
resistance collapsed almost totally and the last Yüan emperor fled in
confusion to the steppes. The Mongol domain in China vanished, so to
speak, in one swoop.

The decisiveness of the Chinese victory over the northern nomads
was not wholly appreciated by the founders of the Ming dynasty. Mop-
up military operations within and outside China proper persisted for
sixty years; and both the later Ming emperors and their Ch'ing dynasty
(1644-1912) successors repeatedly contended with potential or real
Mongol threats on the northern and western frontiers, down into the
eighteenth century. Indeed, it was new non-Chinese overlords from
the north who replaced the Ming dynasty in 1644, but the Manchu founders of the Ch'ing dynasty were not nomadic enemies of the Chinese way
of life. They had profited from a long and unresisting discipleship in
Chinese culture and statecraft before they came to power in China, and
they proposed no alternative to the tradition. Rather, they adopted and
exalted traditional Chinese civilization with zeal--perhaps unfortunately
so, since they ultimately became its rigid defenders when new times
demanded changes. It is therefore clear from today's perspective that
the Chinese way of life after 1368 was not seriously challengeable by
the northerners who had shadowed all its previous history, and the
tension between farmer and nomad was no longer a major theme in
Chinese history.

One major historical tension of Chinese life that did rise into prominence with the establishment of the Ming dynasty was the tension between more absolutist and less absolutist modes of rulership. No one
would seriously suggest that the Chinese have ever experienced even
quasi-democratic rule. From Han into T'ang times, however, the persistence of a semifeudal aristocratic class provided many checks on
imperial power, so that the ruler, while more than a _primus inter_

pares, was not unchallengeably supreme. From T'ang into Sung times this old aristocracy gradually gave way to a prestigious civil service meritocracy, which at times managed to impose institutionalized restraints on the imperial power. Then the Mongols thrust their own variety of aristocratic feudalism on China. When a commoner fought his way to the throne as the first Ming emperor, a host of complex influences came into play: his own strong personality, the remnants of Yüan institutions that confronted him during his rise, what he learned of the pre-Yüan tradition, and modifications made by his immediate successors. These influences combined to produce a distinctive style of rule that modern students have come to call Ming despotism. It provided a capriciously absolutist pattern for Chinese government into our own time.

II. The Transition from Yüan to Ming

The history of the transitional era from Yüan to Ming is compelling drama in its own right, full of action and leavened with moral and political lessons. It begins with deterioration of the Yüan government at all levels and the emergence of colorful regional warlords from unorthodox backgrounds, hostile to one another as well as to the alien government. It culminates in the rise and thirty-year reign of one of the most improbable major figures of all Chinese history, Chu Yüan-chang 朱元璋 -- impoverished orphan, mendicant monk, rebel chieftain, final scourge of the alien overlords, and revered but unloved emperor: Grand Progenitor (T'ai-tsu 太祖, posthumous temple designation) of the Ming dynasty.

Deterioration of Mongol Control

The decline of the Yüan dynasty has sometimes been explained in terms of the dynastic cycle, by which the Chinese have traditionally interpreted their whole history. After the early great khans such as Chingis (Ch'eng-chi-ssu to the Chinese) and Kubilai (Hu-pi-lieh) in the thirteenth century, the vigor of Mongol rulers deteriorated steadily and markedly. The court's ineptitude and inattentiveness allowed abuses to undermine the government's effectiveness. Untalented favorites exploited administration for their selfish ends, intrigues disrupted normal administrative functioning, both military and fiscal preparedness was neglected, and finally, strange natural phenomena followed by natural disasters signaled that Heaven had lost patience with the Mongol rulers, making their overthrow inevitable. All these things are fully documented in the Chinese records, but the modern Chinese have been inclined to treat the Yüan period as a special case, an unfortunate aberration in the normal progression of their history. The Yüan period is now normally depicted in terms of extreme wickedness and cruelty on the part of the Mongols and extreme humiliation and suffering on the part of the Chinese. A catalog of Chinese resentments about their mistreatment under the Mongols is usually offered in lieu of an analysis of Mongol decline.

Chinese resentments were numerous and justified, to be sure. The Mongols consistently treated the Chinese as dregs of the social order, assigning them a status below that of any alien group in China. They disdained the agrarian masses and, even more outrageously, gentlemen of Confucian learning. They enslaved large numbers of Chinese and confiscated their lands, both slaves and lands being handed out as rewards to court favorites. They excluded Chinese from governmental positions except as technicians or clerical assistants. They repeatedly issued orders (no doubt unenforceable, but nevertheless resented) that forbade Chinese to move about freely at night, even to burn lamps in their homes at night, or to assemble for any unsanctioned meeting; to study Mongolian or any other foreign language; to possess arms, to study and practice any military arts, or to hunt even without arms except in small groups. For surveillance and control they organized Chinese into registration groups of twenty households, over each of which an assigned Mongol had dictatorial authority, including the right of sexual intercourse with all young women of the group. One dominant chief councilor (ch'eng-hsiang), Bayan (Pai-yen 伯顏), went so far as to suggest callously in 1337 that trouble with the natives could be minimized if the government would simply put to death all Chinese of the five commonest surnames: Chang, Wang, Liu, Li, and Chao. Had it been carried out, his proposal would have reduced the Chinese population by perhaps half.

In contrast, the Mongols welcomed, trusted, and lavishly patronized non-Mongol aliens in their service, including such adventurers as the Venetian Marco Polo, efficiency experts such as the Persian Ahmad (or Achmach; A-ho-ma 阿合馬) and the Uighur Sengge (or Sanga; Sang-ko 桑哥), and advocates of alien religions such as the Christian John of Montecorvino and, especially, Tibetan lamas such as the creator of a new Mongol script, Phags-pa (Pa-ssu-pa 八思巴). Several Mongol emperors showered vast sums on lamas for support of their temples, shrines, and ceremonies and for copying or printing their voluminous sutras. Lamas accumulated such privileges, wealth, and influence, legally and otherwise, that they became targets of especially virulent Chinese resentments, suggested in the cautionary maxim, "Curse a lama, lose your tongue; strike a lama, lose your arm."

Reading some modern Chinese historians gives the impression that frustrated and ineffectively suppressed rage among the Chinese, aggravated by natural calamities, kept boiling until it just got out of Mongol control. There can be no denying that widespread discontent about the social inequities described above was a catalytic element in the termination of the Yüan dynasty. But deteriorating fiscal and administrative conditions must also be reckoned with.

The Mongols got into fiscal difficulties as early as the reign of Kubilai, when the extended supranational Mongol empire began to break into fragments, so that trade across Central Asia was disrupted, and when resources were depleted by sharing of revenues with rapacious tax farmers and by ambitious enterprises such as unsuccessful invasions of Japan in 1274 and 1281. Throughout the dynasty governmental resources were dissipated by rich gifts to favorites of all sorts and by grants of large tracts of tax-exempt agricultural lands to feudal nobles and religious establishments. Moreover, the central government was vulnerably dependent on grain revenues from the productive Yangtze delta region, from which large flotillas hauled millions of bushels of grain northward each year by sea, around the Shantung peninsula. China's traditional inland canal-transport complex was restored in the 1280s and the 1290s and extended from the Yellow River to Peking; but canal transport was easily disrupted by local disorders and calamitous floods. Sea transport, consequently, remained the fiscal lifeline of the Chinese empire, even though harassed constantly by Japanese raiders, native coastal pirates, and storms. Beginning in the 1340s sea transport became steadily less reliable, and by the mid-1350s grain delivery to the north had virtually ceased. Successive droughts, locust infestations, and military operations in North China in the same period were ruinous. Since food shortages could not be relieved with revenues from the south, endemic famine resulted. There was also runaway inflation of the paper money that the Yüan government had been issuing since 1260. Peking was therefore left with few fiscal resources to cope with threats to dynastic stability.

Administrative stability weakened steadily after Kubilai's time, in a number of aspects. The ruling family was unfortunate in producing a sequence of short-lived, weak-willed, pleasure-loving emperors who could not suppress, and often exacerbated, court intrigues that deflected everyone's attention away from important government business. Two of Kubilai's successors were murdered, victims of struggles for power among court factions, and none distinguished himself as a ruler of China. Important positions in the central government were overwhelmingly occupied by Mongol nobles or other non-Chinese, so that emperors were normally advised by officials who were as out of touch as they themselves were with actual conditions among the people of the empire. At the provincial and regional levels, government was usually dominated by Mongol military commanders, ever ready to take vigorous part in factional strife at court or to behave as autonomous satraps. At the lowest levels, public affairs were dominated by whatever Mongol chiefs, religious establishments, rich merchants, or large landowners happened to be locally most influential. At all levels, offices were often filled on the principle of hereditary succession. Thus, although the formal structure of government was extraordinarily unitary and centralized, in reality administration was fragmented to such a degree that the government had no overall unity. By the middle of the fourteenth century, in consequence, Yüan China was ill prepared even to recognize large-scale problems, much less to deal effectively with them.

The disunity and consequent instability of the Mongol administration in China resulted in part from traditional tribal egalitarianism among the Mongols themselves. But an element at least equally important, and probably much more so, was the failure of the Mongols to create and exploit a large native bureaucracy of the traditional Chinese sort, having strong roots in the native society, a cohesive ideology, and a sense of common cause. The Yüan government did institute civil service examinations beginning in 1315, but they were regulated in such a way that Mongols and other non-Chinese were given simpler tests than Chinese candidates, always won half of all degrees conferred, and got preferential treatment in subsequent consideration for appointments. Although Chinese did attain degree status and some had satisfying governmental careers (in the course of the dynasty two northern Chinese were appointed chief councilor, as was one Central Asian Moslem), their prestige and prospects were severely limited. The general rule was that none but a Mongol could serve as head of any government agency, whether at the capital or in provincial and local administration. In short, the Mongols distrusted the Chinese too much. There is every reason to believe that under more conciliatory circumstances, certainly after the initial shock of the conquest had passed, Chinese would have served the Mongols with sufficient loyalty and effectiveness to avert or significantly moderate the extreme instability of the Yüan government in the 1350s and 1360s.

As things turned out, chaotic disunity is the major historical theme of the final Yüan decades. The last Mongol to reign in Peking, Toghon Temür (T'o-huan T'ieh-mu-erh 妥懽帖睦頤), known most commonly by the posthumous designation Shun-ti 順帝 that was conferred on him by the first Ming emperor, came to the throne in 1333 as a teenager patronized by an empress dowager who was not his own mother. It would probably not be an unreasonable exaggeration to say that his whole reign was devoted to the pursuit of his personal pleasures. Soon after taking the throne he ordered that no young woman over sixteen could be married anywhere in the empire, even in Korea, until he had finished selecting his harem.

In Shun-ti's early years on the throne the government was dominated by the callous chief councilor already mentioned, Bayan. Bayan was powerful enough to punish misbehaving Mongol princes at will; he even had Shun-ti's empress put to death when her brothers were implicated in an alleged treasonable plot. In 1340, however, Bayan was overthrown by his own nephew Toghto (T'o-t'o 脫脫), and he died en route into exile. Toghto remained in power at court until 1354 and seems to have been the last Mongol leader who could organize a large-scale governmental effort of any effectiveness. In 1351 he sent his younger brother Esen Temür (Yeh-hsien T'ieh-mu-erh 也先帖木兒) on campaigns against southern rebels. But Esen Temür was not able to win a decisive victory and in 1352 was humiliatingly defeated near Feng-yang in the northern part of modern Anhwei province, losing vast quantities of military stores. With rebellions raging everywhere and government forces badly demoralized and fragmented, Toghto took the field himself in a series of large-scale campaigns. Commanding a huge force of Mongols, Central Asians, Tibetans, and Koreans as well as Chinese, he brought punishing pressure against the southeastern rebel leader Chang Shih-ch'eng at the strategic city of Kao-yu, north of Yang-chou on the Yangtze. When Toghto was about to prevail, however, he was suddenly dismissed from service and ordered into banishment, victimized by court intrigues on the part of his Secretariat colleague Ha-ma 哈麻 At the same time, Esen Temür was also dismissed from service and banished.

After Toghto's departure from service the Yüan government lacked any semblance of centralized control, and the court was rent by partisan struggles. Two loyalist officers from Honan province, a Mongol named Chaghan Temür (Ch'a-han T'ieh-mu-erh 察罕帖木兒) and a Chinese named Li Ssu-ch'i 李思齊 , raised armies that had some success in restoring order in North China, from Shansi to Shantung, by 1362. In the process Chaghan Temür was murdered by a rebel agent, but his adopted son Kökö Temür (K'uo-k'uo T'ieh-mu-erh 擴廓帖木兒, sometimes rendered K'u-k'u T'ieh-mu-erh 庫庫帖木兒) effectively took his place. Kökö Temür was Chaghan Temür's sororal nephew, a Mongol-Chinese halfbreed originally named Wang Pao-pao 王保保; Shun-ti had granted him a Mongol name when his uncle adopted him. Antagonisms between Kökö Temür and the Mongol commander in Shansi province, a veteran campaigner against rebels named Balod Temür (Po-lo T'ieh-mu-erh 孛羅帖木兒), were soon exploited by contending factions at court.

At this critical time, in 1363, Shun-ti's second empress, a Korean woman surnamed Ki (Ch'i 奇) and her son, the officially designated heir apparent Ayushiridara (Ai-yu-shih-li-ta-la 愛猷識理達臘, were plotting to coerce Shun-ti into abdication. One of their clients at court, the chief councilor Ch'o-ssu-chien 搠思監, was feuding with the censor-in-chief Lao-ti-sha 老的沙. Ayushiridara persuaded Shun-ti to dismiss Lao-ti-sha, who then fled for protection to Balod Temür. Ch'o-ssu-chien promptly denounced Balod Temür as a traitor, whereupon Balod Temür in fact revolted, assaulted Peking, and put to death both Ch'o-ssu-chien and a powerful Korean eunuch who was Empress Ki's principal agent. Ayushiridara fled for help to Kökö Temür, who responded by marching his army in turn upon Peking and taking effective control of the capital in 1365. Balod Temür died at the hands of an assassin. Kökö Temür resisted Ayushiridara's persuasions that he depose Shun-ti by force and instead accepted from Shun-ti a princely title and a commission to organize all Yüan military forces in a massive campaign to destroy the rebellious groups along the Yangtze. This undertaking ran into immediate troubles in 1366, however, for both Li Ssu-ch'i in Honan province and Chang Liang-pi 張良弼 (also referred to as Chang Ssu-tao 張思道), a Chinese commander of Yüan forces in Shensi province, resented Kökö Temür's rise to preeminence and combined to attack him. While Kökö Temür was trying to put down this insurrection, the heir apparent Ayushiridara prevailed upon Shun-ti to order Kökö Temür's dismissal, and Ayushiridara himself was named generalissimo of the Yüan forces in 1367. Such was the bizarre succession of events that allowed native rebels to erect regional states along the Yangtze in defiance of Peking in the 1350s and 1360s and finally to overrun North China in 1368.

Rebellions of the 1350s and 1360s

The character of Chinese history in the last years of the Yüan dynasty has been described aptly by F. W. Mote as follows:

About the middle of the fourteenth century a strange collection of men became the leading figures on the stage of

Chinese history. They were in almost no way characteristic
of the actors who usually dominated that stage. It was as if
the proper drama had paused for a long intermission, during
which a whole arena of character players and minor stars were
allowed to occupy stage front and center. These proved to be
a motley assortment of thieves and villains, ruffians and ras-
cals, clowns and bit players. The main drama gave way
temporarily to what seemed to be a talent show for amateurs,
a chaos of smaller acts.[1]

Among the actors who now took the stage were men of principle
and vision who hoped to create new imperial regimes and, on the other
hand, mere troublemakers who had neither the boldness nor the imagi-
nation to become empire builders. What gave all of them an opportunity
to catapult themselves into prominence, aside from the general discontent and decay that have been previously described, was a massive call-
up of peasants to work on the Yellow River in 1351, after its floodwaters
spread disastrously throughout the Huai River basin along the central
part of China's east coast, from the Shantung peninsula south toward the
Yangtze delta. This region is naturally swampy, unappealing, and poor.
Moreover, its historic role had long been to serve as a battle-ravaged
no-man's-land between North and South, and it had suffered severely
during the Sung dynasty's resistance first against the Jurchen Chin
dynasty in the twelfth century and then against the Mongols in the thirteenth. When floods overwhelmed it and the Yüan government called
out its residents in hundreds of thousands to do burdensome corvée
labor on the ruined waterways complex, the region became the epi-
center of rebellious waves that eventually shook apart the Mongol
empire.

One major late Yüan protagonist was already on the stage far to the
south. This was Fang Kuo-chen 方國珍 (1319/20-1374), whose forebears had long been fishermen and coastal salt traders in T'ai-chou
prefecture of modern Chekiang province. The salt trade was a lucra-
tive one traditionally monopolized by Chinese governments since ancient
times, and those who engaged in it often teetered between legitimate
trade and smuggling. Like many more or less respectable people of
the area, Fang as a young man apparently engaged in illegal profiteering,
which brought him to the verge of arrest in 1348. To avoid trouble Fang
fled to sea as a pirate, and a large following of bullies and toughs
quickly gathered around him. The Yüan government, adopting centuries-
old Chinese ways of dealing with such nuisances, tried to mollify him
with grants of petty military titles in the pretence that he was part of the
official coastal defense system, but Fang continued to seize favorable

opportunities to raid government fleets carrying grain northward from the Yangtze delta.

Widespread rebellions provoked by the 1351 troubles in the Huai River basin, by forcing the government to draw much of its naval strength into inland waters, especially along the Yangtze, gave Fang Kuo-chen almost complete freedom of action along the coast. Between 1352 and 1360 his fleet grew to more than a thousand vessels, which effectively dominated the whole Chekiang coast south of Hangchow Bay. He toyed with the government, "surrendering" for ever higher rewards and titles or alternatively rebelling, as suited his convenience.

A strong and threatening sea raider, Fang Kuo-chen never seems to have made a serious effort to create and expand an important land base. In 1354 and 1355, however, taking advantage of the confused situation in the interior, he captured three important prefectural cities on the Chekiang coast: T'ai-chou, Ning-po, and Wen-chou; and in 1358 he temporarily added to his domain the most important city on the south side of Hangchow Bay, Shao-hsing. In central and southern Chekiang he was the unchallenged warlord through most of the 1360s. Fang had to be warily unprovocative, however, in his relations with Yüan loyalists to the south in Fukien province and with rebel leaders on his north, in the Yangtze delta, and on his west in the central Yangtze area. His opportunistically exploitive relationship with the Yüan government eventually brought him recognition as the legitimate governor of his Chekiang domain (grandiosely called Huai-nan, implying the whole area south of the Huai basin), hereditary status as a duke, and the honorific title grand marshal (t'ai-wei), in exchange for which he inconsistently dispatched token grain shipments to the north.

*   *   *   *   *

Among the rebel leaders who appeared in the Huai area after the 1351 floods was a more ambitious man than Fang Kuo-chen, named Chang Shih-ch'eng 張士誠 (1321-1367). Like Fang, Chang had a salt trade background. Native to the Kao-yu region of modern Kiangsu province, north of the Yangtze, Chang and his brothers grew up as canal boatmen employed by the state salt monopoly. It was the common fate of such lowly workers to be oppressed and cheated by both functionaries and wealthy families, and the Chang brothers were exceptional only in that they were unsubmissive to such treatment. Chang Shih-ch'eng formed a small group of friends who were determined to strike back at their tormenters and perhaps, in the process, make their fortunes. Soon, after several acts of arson, Chang found himself an outlaw. Allies were easy to rally from among the impoverished people of the vicinity. With their help Chang easily fought off a militia force organized by wealthy towns-people and then quickly took control of the two nearest cities, T'ai-chou (not to be confused with Fang Kuo-chen's T'ai-chou far to the south) and Hsing-hua. Yüan officials tried to appease him with the offer of a civil service appointment, which he spurned. He gathered together more bandits and rebels, and in 1353 captured Kao-yu itself, situated strate-gically on the Grand Canal.

Chang Shih-ch'eng promptly established a strong base at Kao-yu and proclaimed himself prince of a new state bearing the ancient and auspicious dynastic name Chou. He successfully resisted both appease-ment efforts and assaults by the Yüan government. When Toghto's massive 1354 campaign against him was aborted by court intrigues, large numbers of Yüan troops joined Chang's cause, and he gained con-trol over an extensive part of Kiangsu province north of the Yangtze. He seemed content with this situation until 1356, when a severe famine scattered other rebellious forces out of the Huai basin and drove him out as well. Abandoning Kao-yu, he moved southward and across the Yangtze into the south-bank city Chiang-yin. Then his forces quickly overran the highly productive, prosperous, and elegant Yangtze delta area traditionally called Chiang-nan, dominated now by Shanghai on the coast but then by the inland metropolis Soochow.

From his new capital at Soochow, Chang Shih-ch'eng extended his authority over northern Chekiang. In 1357 the other great southeastern metropolis, Hangchow, surrendered to him without a fight, and soon thereafter he displaced his southern rival Fang Kuo-chen from Shao-hsing, across Hangchow Bay. Meanwhile, under pressure on other fronts from both Yüan and other rebel forces, Chang had nominally made peace with the government in exchange for the honorific title grand marshal and legitimation of his de facto role as ruler of the Yangtze delta. From 1359 to 1363 he even sent token grain shipments north to the Yüan capital in uneasy collaboration with Fang Kuo-chen, who was also temporarily at peace with the Mongols and provided the necessary transport ships. But in 1363 Chang grew bolder. Denouncing the Yüan, he again set himself up as an independent prince, this time naming his state Wu, a prideful designation for the Soochow region since antiquity. He built a palace and created a state bureaucracy, both on an imperial scale; and his forces began pushing back to the north against rival reb-els, extending his domain as far as Hsü-chou in far northern Kiangsu, near the border of Shantung province.

Unlike his southern rival Fang Kuo-chen, Chang Shih-ch'eng was more than an adventurous plunderer. Despite his lowly origins, he had imperial pretensions and, in adapting to the elegant atmosphere of Soochow, developed an air of imperial refinement. He seems to have undertaken the obligations of rulership seriously and conscientiously: he sought out learned advisers and listened to them; he tried to maintain a trustworthy administration by suppressing corruption in his bureaucracy; and he disciplined his troops so that they did not prey on the people. Since his state of Wu was the most stubborn obstacle to the ultimate emergence of the new dynasty based at Nanking to the west, official Ming records depict Chang and his followers maliciously, as slothful and effete incompetents, but a somewhat idealizing sentimentalism about Chang persisted in Soochow into modern times. On balance, it would appear that Chang's military strength did deteriorate after 1357 in the relatively luxurious delta environment; that Chang endured incompetence among his administrators too leniently; and that he himself gradually lost whatever original determination he may have had to prevail over all his enemies and rivals: he became too genteel for that. He lacked the unrelenting toughness that was required to win the empire in the 1360s.

*   *   *   *   *

While Chang Shih-ch'eng and Fang Kuo-chen were setting up their satrapies in the Yangtze delta and on the southeastern coast, rebel leaders of a different character were spreading northward and westward out of the Huai basin and the central Yangtze region. Although basically no doubt as opportunistic as Chang and Fang, they were united in a loose confederation paying at least lip service to the religious cause of visionaries who for centuries had been proclaiming the imminent appearance of a messianic savior who would transform Chinese state and society into a paradise of political justice, social equity, and general economic prosperity. Their heritage, foreshadowing the Taiping and Boxer movements of the nineteenth century, combined heterogeneous folk-religion elements with secret-society tactics. They flourished particularly in the oppressive atmosphere of Yüan times, when populist underground movements were of three principal sorts, confusingly intermixed. One was the Maitreya sect (Mi-lo chiao 彌勒教), a militant branch of original Pure Land Buddhism, having especially strong roots in southeastern China. Second was a subgroup of this, the even more militant White Lotus sect (Pai-lien chiao 白蓮教), devoted to the service of the god of light, Amida Buddha, which by Yüan times had long been dominated by the Han family of modern Hopei province, on the North China plain. The third ingredient was Manichaeism (Ming chiao 明教, a fusing of Zoroastrian, Christian, Buddhist, and Taoist influences that had been known in China since T'ang times, had become particularly entrenched in the southeast, and in Yüan times was being absorbed by the Maitreya and White Lotus sects. All three movements engaged in elaborate incense-burning ceremonies and identified their adherents by the wearing of red headbands. Rebels of these sorts were therefore commonly called Red Turbans (hung-chin 紅巾), the Red Army (hung-chün 紅軍), or the Incense Army (hsiang-chün 香軍).

Red Turban rebels arose in the Huai basin in 1351 in support of a boy named Han Lin-erh 韓林兒, reputed to be not only the awaited Manichaean-Buddhist savior, and hence called the Little Prince of Brightness (hsiao ming wang 小明王), but also the legitimate heir of the defunct but revered Sung dynasty. Under the generalship of a local leader named Liu Fu-t'ung 劉福通, the Red Turbans soon seized the northern Anhwei town Po-chou, where after surviving Yüan efforts to suppress them they established Han Lin-erh as emperor of a revived Sung dynasty in 1355. The rebellion attracted widespread support throughout North China, and in 1358 Liu Fu-t'ung led forces triumphantly into the old Sung capital Kaifeng, in the central Yellow River plain. At the same time, one of his columns pushed northwestward into Shensi and Shansi and another pushed northeastward into Shantung. The latter force was eventually suppressed by the Mongol-Chinese general Kökö Temür in the early 1360s. The former force roamed extensively through Shensi and Shansi, then moved far northward to ransack the Mongols' extra-mural capital Shang-tu, in modern Chahar province, and then moved far eastward into the modern Liaotung region, where Mongols eventually exterminated it also.

Meanwhile, Han Lin-erh and Liu Fu-t'ung were driven out of Kaifeng in 1359 by the Yüan loyalist Chaghan Temür and withdrew to An-feng in far northwestern Anhwei province. There they maintained nominal control over the still widespread rebel movement until 1363, when Chang Shih-ch'eng's forces, in their belated northern expansion, captured An-feng and killed Liu Fu-t'ung. Han Lin-erh fled into the camp of his nominal subordinate Chu Yüan-chang, under whose patronage he retained his imperial pretensions at Ch'u-chou, an important city in east central Anhwei, until his death in 1366.

A loosely allied Red Turban movement was simultaneously taking control of the central and western Yangtze regions. Whereas the northern Red Turbans were predominantly under White Lotus influence, these western rebels were predominantly Maitreya worshippers. Their original organizer was a monk named P'eng Ying-yü 彭瑩玉, who had been agitating in the southeast and the Huai basin for some fifteen years before 1351, when he helped an ineffectual but handsome cloth peddler named Hsü Shou-hui 徐壽輝 to lead a successful uprising in Ch'i-shui, in modern Hupei province not far from the Anhwei border, north of the Yangtze. Never a close collaborator with the Han Lin-erh group, Hsü from the beginning had imperial pretensions of his own and set up an independent Red Turban state called T'ien-wan 天完. Hsü himself was, however, a weakling manipulated by militant supporters, whose rivalries kept the T'ien-wan state poorly organized even though its domain spread extensively. The early strongman of the regime was Ni Wen-chün 倪文俊, originally a fisherman. Within a year T'ien-wan forces controlled the central Yangtze regions and portions of the southeast; they even occupied the east coast metropolis Hangchow briefly in 1352. Thereafter, from a base area incorporating large parts of modern Hupei, Hunan, and Kiangsi provinces, their thrust was mainly westward up the Yangtze and its tributaries. By 1356 T'ien-wan was under pressure from rival rebel regimes in the east, and Hsü Shou-hui moved his capital west to a more central location at Han-yang, at the confluence of the Han River with the Yangtze.

Ni Wen-chün was murdered in 1357 by a favored subordinate, Ch'en Yu-liang 陳友諒 (1320/21-1363). Ch'en was also of fisherman background but had been serving in a petty local government clerical position when the Red Turbans erupted in 1351. Joining them, he had quickly gained military strength and reputation. After murdering Ni Wen-chün, he became the preeminent military leader of T'ien-wan but had to murder another colleague in 1359 to consolidate his power. He then set up his own regional state of Han with its capital at Chiang-chou (modern Kiukiang) on the Yangtze in Kiangsi province, east of Han-yang. Hsü Shou-hui promptly moved his T'ien-wan imperial capital there, only to be murdered on Ch'en's orders in 1360. Ch'en then took the title emperor for himself.

By this time the original T'ien-wan domain was threatening to break up. The principal defector was Ming Yü-chen 明玉珍 (1331-1366), a Hunanese commoner who had early led a local uprising that was incorporated into Hsü Shou-hui's movement in 1352. Beginning in 1357, as a local T'ien-wan commander west of the capital at Han-yang, he had subjugated Szechwan province virtually on his own initiative, and Hsü Shou-hui had officially designated him governor of Szechwan and Shensi in 1359. When Ch'en Yu-liang murdered Hsü Shou-hui in 1360, Ming Yü-chen set up an independent western state that came to be known by the ancient legendary dynastic name Hsia. He proclaimed ambitions to conquer the whole empire, fostered Confucian thought and learning, instituted imperial-style civil service examinations, and seems to have ruled his domain benevolently; but he died in 1366 while only thirty-five years old, probably murdered. His young son, Ming Sheng 明昇 , came to the Hsia throne supported by his mother and the general Wu Yu-jen 吳友仁 ; but the Hsia state, troubled by court factionalism and local separatist inclinations, no longer prospered.

The defection of Szechwan under Ming Yü-chen did not seriously weaken Ch'en Yu-liang's Han state in the central Yangtze region; but Ch'en was seriously threatened by the rise of Chu Yüan-chang to power on his northeast, in the area of modern Nanking. Ch'en tried to arouse Chang Shih-ch'eng in Soochow to join a pincers action against Chu, but in vain. After some unsuccessful sorties of his own, Ch'en had to abandon his most easterly territories to Chu and in 1361 fell back to the Han-yang area. There he revived and reorganized his forces, and in 1362 he launched a great naval expedition down the Yangtze against Chu. This culminated in a critical and famous series of engagements on Poyang Lake in Kiangsi province, in which Ch'en's force was finally routed and Ch'en was killed. Although Ch'en's young heir was enthroned as the new Han emperor, his state was disintegrating.

The Rise of Chu Yüan-chang

Chu Yüan-chang was one of the men who gained regional power under the aegis of the northern Red Turbans. His forebears had long been lower-class artisans of the Yangtze basin, but in the Yüan period they had moved into the Huai basin and become tenant farmers. His father, Chu Shih-chen 朱世珍, had proved particularly unsuccessful and had moved about repeatedly in northeastern and north central Anhwei. Chu Yüan-chang, born in 1328 as the last of six children, was regularly hired out as a cowherd while a boy. Both his sisters and one of his three older brothers married and left home while he was still quite young. His two other brothers had unfortunate marriages: their wives and children all died early. Crushing disaster finally hit the family in 1344, when famine and plague ravaged the area around modern Feng-yang and Chu's father, mother, and eldest brother all died in quick succession. The two surviving sons, landless and penniless, borrowed land in which to give their dead crude burials, and then sixteen-year-old Chu Yüan-chang was deposited with a small nearby Buddhist monastery as a lay novice, the polite term for a menial servant.

Economic conditions worsened so steadily that before two months
had passed young Chu was turned out of the monastery, which could no
longer support its staff, to make his way as best he could in the role of
a mendicant monk. For more than three years he thus wandered about
the Huai basin, becoming thoroughly acquainted with the terrain, the
people, and the troubles of the region. It is possible he participated in
some Red Turban agitations at this time; P'eng Ying-yü and Liu Fu-
t'ung were already preaching and prowling through the region. Certainly, young Chu must have lived off his wits as much as out of his
begging bowl. Then in 1348, at the age of twenty, he was readmitted to
his old monastery and began acquiring some rudimentary education. He
was apparently pursuing his Buddhist studies peaceably when rebellions
burst out into the open throughout the region in 1351.

One of the early branch headquarters of the widespread Red Turban
movement was Feng-yang city, then called Hao-chou. This was the base
of Kuo Tzu-hsing 郭子興, scion of a well-to-do family of fortune
tellers originally from Shantung. Close friends of Chu Yüan-chang were
among Kuo's associates, and they promptly began urging Chu to join
them. In later life Chu recollected that he was very hesitant to do so;
but he was a tall, robust, experienced young man who could hardly have
been a very devout ascetic, and his instincts must have inclined him
toward a more active life. Moreover, the Yüan government, though lax
in suppressing the organized rebels, began intimidating defenseless
Buddhist monasteries where rebellious doctrines might have been propa-
gated. Chu's own little sanctuary was finally burned down in this campaign. But by that time, with the help of Buddhist meditations and divi-
nations, Chu had already made up his mind to join the rebels at Hao-
chou, where he appeared in the spring of 1352.

From the outset the Hao-chou movement was weakened by intrigues
among the leaders, for which Kuo Tzu-hsing had a strong propensity.
When Chu Yüan-chang arrived, Kuo, and especially his strong-willed
wife, saw in him potentially powerful support for themselves; for in
addition to being big and strong Chu had a tough and mean look, with
a heavy protruding jaw, that somewhat awed others. Kuo took Chu into
his camp as a kind of personal orderly, and Kuo's wife arranged for
Chu to marry an orphaned Miss Ma 馬 who had become Kuo's ward.
Chu's new wife proved to be strong-willed herself and was a powerful
influence on him throughout his rise to power. She, Kuo's wife, and
Chu soon became an indomitable combination supporting Kuo against
his challengers within the rebel group.

In 1353 Chu was sent out to recruit new followers in the villages around his home, and he returned to Hao-chou with some seven hundred men whose principal loyalty was to himself. These included his boyhood friends Hsü Ta 徐達 and T'ang Ho 湯和, who were eventually to rank among the great early Ming generals. In the following year, tiring of the Hao-chou intrigues, Chu got permission to strike out on forays of his own and captured the town of Ting-yüan to the south. There he gained more than twenty thousand new militiamen adherents and two influential advisers, the well-to-do landowner Feng Kuo-yung 馮國用 and the scholar Li Shan-ch'ang 李善長 . Feng urged Chu to concentrate on capturing the great central Yangtze power center Nanking, from which the whole empire might be subjugated; and Li began counseling him to emulate the tough-minded but benevolent founder of the Han dynasty in the third century B.C., the only commoner who had ever fought his way to the throne of all China. Thus encouraged and reinforced, Chu moved eastward and subdued Ch'u-chou, an important trade center in east central Anhwei, where his fraternal nephew Chu Wen-cheng 朱文正 and his sororal nephew Li Wen-chung 李文忠 joined him with the news that they were now the only survivors of the original family.

From Ch'u-chou late in 1354 Chu Yüan-chang responded to an appeal from the rival rebel Chang Shih-ch'eng, then under assault by Toghto Temür in Kao-yu, by rushing east into modern Kiangsu to relieve a Mongol siege of the town Liu-ho, part of Chang's domain. Then in 1355, when food supplies in the Ch'u-chou area seemed unlikely to provide for his growing army, Chu moved on southward, to Ho-chou on the north bank of the Yangtze near the modern Anhwei-Kiangsu border. There he was joined by yet another young man who would soon become a famous general, Ch'ang Yü-ch'un 常遇春 .

It was in 1355 that the Red Turban figurehead Han Lin-erh, to whom Kuo Tzu-hsing and Chu Yüan-chang gave allegiance, was proclaimed emperor of Sung with his capital in northern Anhwei. Kuo Tzu-hsing soon died, having already become heavily dependent on Chu's support to retain nominal authority over the Red Turban wing based at Hao-chou. Thereupon, ignoring the fact that Chu had for some time been the most powerful military leader on the southern front, Han Lin-erh named one of Kuo's sons commander-in-chief (tu yüan-shuai) in Chu's area. Chu bided his time. That summer Chinese naval commanders in Yüan service on the Yangtze were induced to defect, and Chu used their ships to move his Red Turban forces across the river into position for taking the strategic town T'ai-p'ing, upriver some fifty miles from

Nanking. Then the rebel army made a premature assault on Nanking, which was well-defended, and suffered heavy losses. The commander-in-chief, Kuo Tzu-hsing's heir, was captured and put to death. The surviving rebels then acclaimed Chu Yüan-chang their new commander-in-chief, and at the age of twenty-seven he was prepared to press forward along his increasingly ambitious path with a now solidly united following.

In late 1355 and early 1356 Chu Yüan-chang's forces devoted themselves to careful clearing away of Yüan defenses upriver, downriver, and inland, steadily isolating Nanking on all but its northeast side. Then in the spring of 1356 Chu sent both river and land forces in three massive assaults on Nanking. When the city wall was finally breached the defenders capitulated, and Chu had control of a strategic metropolis. Han Lin-erh gave him high rank in the rebel Sung government's Bureau of Military Affairs and made him chief of a new Branch Secretariat for the Chiang-nan Area. Li Shan-ch'ang became his principal civil-government aide.

Chu Yüan-chang presented himself to the people of Nanking as a liberator. To a mass gathering of local officials and citizens he proclaimed:

> I have led my host here only to rid you of trouble. Each of
> you should go about your affairs peaceably and unafraid.
> Those among your worthy gentlemen who are able to give
> us meritorious service I shall employ respectfully. You
> who hold office must not maliciously harm the people. I
> shall relieve you of the wrongs of the former administra-
> tion.[2]

In many ways Chu tried to give substance to this image. He welcomed and listened to men of learning, placed men he trusted and respected in charge of the localities under his control, and indoctrinated his generals and soldiers not to kill needlessly and, above all, not to plunder and rape among the people. "Whenever people submit, we must make them happy and not take a single thing. In this fashion everyone will press forward zealously, and there will be no place that we cannot take, no battle that we cannot win."[3] As his forces spread out to secure the approaches to Nanking, his reputation as a benevolent liberator commanding disciplined troops proved to be one of his greatest assets; Chinese villagers and townspeople, including those in Yüan military service whose duty was to destroy him, were increasingly in a mood to welcome him without resistance.

Chu was especially attracted to the ancient Chinese system of military colonies (t'un-t'ien) in which soldiers rotated between military activities and working government-provided farms for their own sustenance. In 1358 he ordered adoption of this system throughout all his armies, in the hope of making them self-sufficient and not a burden on the civilian population.

Chu Yüan-chang was fortunate in having several years at this juncture to consolidate his position and create a stable administration at Nanking relatively undisturbed. Chang Shih-ch'eng and Fang Kuo-chen were simultaneously establishing themselves to the east and southeast. The Red Turbans of Hsü Shou-hui, and later Ch'en Yu-liang, were occupied to the west in Hunan, Hupei, and Szechwan. Yüan forces in the far south, cut off from Peking by the Yangtze rebellions and distracted by local disorders, were beyond the natural shield of the rugged Kiangsi-Kwangtung mountains. The northern Red Turbans dominated the region between Chu's domain and Peking, so that there was no Yüan threat from the north. Chu's forces nevertheless were not idle. Between 1356 and 1359, while establishing and maintaining a strong defensive posture to the west confronting the western Red Turbans, they steadily expanded Chu's domain eastward into Kiangsu and Chekiang, creating a defensive line that protected Nanking from Chang Shih-ch'eng at Soochow. In 1359 Fang Kuo-chen, on the Chekiang coast, was even persuaded to give Chu his nominal allegiance. While engaged in these campaigns in Chekiang in 1358, Chu became acquainted with two of the most gifted litterateurs of the time, Sung Lien 宋濂 and Liu Chi 劉基 , both of whom he induced to join his staff. Under their tutelage, Chu assiduously studied the Confucian classics, learned about traditional Chinese ways of government, and enticed still more notables into his service.

In 1360 Chu Yüan-chang's respite was terminated by challenges from Ch'en Yu-liang on his west. Ch'en began encroaching aggressively on Chu's territory; he took T'ai-p'ing and launched an assault on Nanking but was beaten back with many losses. By now, less and less inspired by his nominal emperor Han Lin-erh to the north, Chu was cautiously developing his own imperial ambitions and knew that his next step must be to dispose of both his Yangtze rivals, Chang Shih-ch'eng as well as Ch'en Yu-liang. He calculated that Chang, though rich in material resources, was less bellicose than Ch'en--that if Chu were to attack Chang, Ch'en would hurl all his strength against Chu's rear, whereas if Chu were to attack Ch'en, Chang would take no significant advantage of the opportunity. Chu calculated correctly. In 1361, without interference from Chang, he marshaled his forces in a campaign straight upriver against Ch'en's capital, Chiang-chou. Ch'en fell back in defeat to the Han-yang area, and Chu's forces took over town after town in northern Kiangsi and eastern Hupei while Ch'en tried to regroup. Han Lin-erh rewarded Chu Yüan-chang with the prestigious title duke of Wu.

In early 1363, while Chu's forces were completing their occupation of the eastern part of Ch'en Yu-liang's Han state, Chang Shih-ch'eng did rouse his forces into action, but not against Chu directly. Instead, they spread north from the Yangtze into Chang's original base area in the Huai basin, crossed west into Anhwei, and laid siege to Han Lin-erh's capital at An-feng. The rebel Sung regime's fortunes had been sharply declining under pressure from Chaghan Temür's armies on the North China plain. Nevertheless, against the advice of such counselors as Liu Chi, Chu Yüan-chang immediately suspended operations in the west and personally led an army to the relief of An-feng, considering it a military necessity to check Chang Shih-ch'eng. Breaking the siege, he took responsibility for the now forlorn Han Lin-erh. Showing him full imperial honor, Chu established him with a palace suite at his own old base, Ch'u-chou. There Han Lin-erh languished under Chu's polite patronage until Han's death late in 1366 by drowning, perhaps engineered by Chu.

Chu Yüan-chang later admitted it was unwise on his part to divert his attention from Ch'en Yu-liang so as to rescue Han Lin-erh; the risks were great. Although Ch'en was hard pressed he was by no means broken. Before the end of 1362 he had begun organizing a new offensive against Chu. With a fleet of more than a hundred large, multi-tiered ships, the largest of which were armor-plated and carried his whole court retinue, Ch'en pressed down the Yangtze and then into vast Poyang Lake in northern Kiangsi province, whose environs had just been occupied by Chu's forces. The greatest city of the area, Nan-ch'ang near the southern end of the lake, was besieged for almost three months but resisted stubbornly under the command of Chu Yüan-chang's nephew Chu Wen-cheng. Ch'en Yu-liang's apparent intent was to clear out such pockets of Chu's strength along the Yangtze to prevent interference from the rear as he proceeded on to Nanking, but his lingering in Poyang Lake gave Chu Yüan-chang time to return from his An-feng campaign, reorganize, and take a large naval force of his own westward up the Yangtze. In late summer of 1363 Chu led his fleet into the northern end of Poyang Lake. Only then did Ch'en break off his siege of Nan-ch'ang to the south to engage Chu in what became the climactic military engagement in the history of the Yüan-to-Ming transition, and probably the greatest naval engagement of all Chinese history.

Traditional accounts credit Ch'en Yu-liang with a force of six hundred thousand men on Poyang Lake. Chu Yüan-chang's force was smaller, and his ships were smaller though more maneuverable than Ch'en's. It seems probable that a total of nearly a million men were involved in this great confrontation, which extended over thirty-six days. Both long-range and short-range bows, fire catapults and other kinds of ballistae, and rude cannons were employed; boarding parties moved back and forth in hand-to-hand combat. Casualties seem to have been enormous on both sides. Chu's commanders repeatedly lost heart, and morale among Ch'en's forces must have been worse. After one early and inconclusive four-day engagement involving both sides at full strength, Ch'en Yu-liang began evading large-scale battles, hiding in protective bays while Chu Yüan-chang's smaller ships taunted the enemy to come out and fight. As days passed with minor skirmishing, Ch'en's supplies dwindled and it became imperative that he break through Chu's fleet and get out of the lake. On October 3 he consequently led his full remaining fleet northward in an effort to regain the Yangtze. In the end Ch'en's large ships successfully smashed Chu's blockade between the lake and the river, but at the crucial hour a strong northeastern wind arose behind Chu. Setting a number of small ships afire, he drove them into Ch'en's massed fleet, and a holocaust ensued that virtually annihilated Ch'en's force. Ch'en himself was hit by an arrow and died. Some of Ch'en's ships fought on in the Yangtze before surrendering, and some of Ch'en's generals escaped westward with his young heir. But after the defeat at the mouth of Poyang Lake Ch'en's state of Han was doomed. By the end of 1363 Chu Yüan-chang had the Han leaders besieged at Wu-ch'ang, across the river from Han-yang; and early the next year they surrendered.

In 1364, having become master of the whole central Yangtze area, Chu Yüan-chang took the title prince of Wu--the same title Chang Shih-ch'eng had assumed the year before. Although Chu continued to render appropriate homage to his nominal emperor Han Lin-erh, he also began establishing an imperial-scale officialdom at Nanking. Meanwhile, his armies without much difficulty consolidated control over the former Han state territories. Late in 1365 his marshals Hsü Ta and Ch'ang Yü-ch'un undertook a major campaign eastward to clear out Chang Shih-ch'eng's strongholds in the Huai basin. This task completed, they moved into the heart of Chang's domain in the Yangtze delta late in 1366. By the end of that year both Hu-chou, south of Lake T'ai, and Hangchow had surrendered and Chang's capital at Soochow was under siege. This siege was long and very hard on the Soochow residents. It was not until October 1367 that the city fell. Chang was thereupon taken captive to Nanking, where he disdainfully rebuffed all overtures and was cruelly put to death.

*   *   *   *   *

Chu Yüan-chang's successful efforts to gain control of central China can be explained in part by the shortcomings of his rivals. Some reasons for Chang Shih-ch'eng's eventual failure despite his having an excellent logistical base have already been suggested. Ch'en Yu-liang's failure is easier to understand. Although the western Red Turban movement gained control over extensive territories that were well endowed materially, had a strategically located base in the dead center of China, and was supported by huge armies renowned for their tough fighting qualities, it proved inept in organizing its material and human resources into a stable, cohesive movement. It was troubled constantly by local separatist movements and by defections to rival rebels. Ch'en Yu-liang himself, though a fearsome political manipulator and battle commander, nevertheless did not impress contemporaries as a likely emperor-to-be. Chu Yüan-chang, however, did not win the empire simply by default; and it was precisely the undefinable charismatic personality of the unchallengeable Great Man, at whose coming one instinctively stands aside alertly and with some sense of danger, that accounted for his success. He was China's comman man writ large: strong, stolid, shrewd, and in some degree fearsomely unpredictable. Although subordinates occasionally defected to the more genteel Chang Shih-ch'eng in search of a less arduous life, those who knew the adult Chu were aware of his determination to prevail and apparently accepted without question the inevitability that he would become emperor.

Some particular qualities and circumstances that aided Chu can be enumerated. He planned his campaigns carefully; saw to it that his troops were trained, supplied, and not abused; and was seldom rash. He was compassionate toward the people at large and toward surrendering enemy soldiers, exuding an air of protective and benevolent leadership. Although he easily became impatient with rhetorical flourishes on the part of the learned, he treated scholars respectfully, attended to the lessons of history seriously, and both sought and heeded guidance and remonstrance that had the ring of pragmatic soundness. He was prudent and proper in relations with his nominal superiors such as Kuo Tzu-hsing and Han Lin-erh, giving no sign of subservience and yet not appearing insubordinate. In personal conduct he seems to have been relatively austere by contemporaneous standards; and without being flamboyant he could rage when aroused. Moreover, it is by no means unimportant that he enjoyed the personal loyalty of extraordinarily capable military commanders such as Ch'ang Yü-ch'un and especially his boyhood friends Hsü Ta and T'ang Ho, whom he trusted to act largely on their own initiative without meddling interference from him.

In short, it might be said that Chu Yüan-chang had the advantages of a corps of talented subordinates of unquestioned loyalty, armies of disciplined but well-treated soldiers, and an austere and awesome public image. His principal base at Nanking also happened to be advantageously situated on a productive plain and astride the most important communication and transport lines of central and eastern China. Even with a relatively small domain sandwiched between the rich and populous domains of Chang Shih-ch'eng and Ch'en Yu-liang, he could never have been reckoned a minor contender. As events proved, he had the persistence and toughness to be the winner.

Expulsion of the Mongols

After the death of Han Lin-erh at the end of 1366, Chu Yüan-chang at last abandoned the pretence of supporting Han's Sung dynasty. Like other rebels, he had for years been plied with offers of high office and other bribes if only he would give even nominal allegiance to the Yüan empire. While declining such offers, he had remained politely deferential toward the Yüan Mongols and on several occasions had released Yüan loyalists who fell into his hands. He had not spent much effort denouncing the Yüan government, but instead had presented himself publicly as a humble man whom circumstances had forced into action to restore order. With Han Lin-erh's death, his power having grown enormously at the expense of Ch'en Yu-liang's regime, Chu ceased using the era-name established by Han Lin-erh and allowed the rebel Sung dynasty to terminate. That he did not perpetuate the rebel Sung dynasty in the role of second emperor, with a new era-name, is significant. We do not know if Chu felt any anguish about what to do next. No doubt he was relieved to be free of the association with Han Lin-erh, which had eventually proved neither advantageous nor prestigious; and the scale of his own personal ambitions may have prevented his accepting the historic role of a second emperor. On the other hand, for whatever reasons, he did not yet feel it appropriate to declare himself first emperor of another dynasty. He merely retained his title as prince of Wu, and the year 1367 is known to history ambiguously, and rather abnormally, as the first year of Wu. After the subjugation of Chang Shih-ch'eng, however, with the whole Yangtze valley from the Szechwan border to the sea in his control, Chu Yüan-chang at last openly proclaimed his determination to eradicate the Yüan dynasty and establish a new dynasty called Ming. The next year, 1368, was to be known as the beginning of an era auspiciously called Hung-wu 洪武 (suggesting "vast martial achievement"). In a proclamation to the empire he accepted the traditionalistic idea that the Mongols could only have conquered China by the mandate of Heaven, argued that the early Yüan rulers and officials had been wise and enlightened but that conditions later became intolerable, and announced that Mongols and other non-Chinese who wished to remain in China would be treated sympathetically.

Many modern historians, both Chinese and Western, would like to interpret the establishment of the Ming dynasty as a popular uprising of at least quasi-nationalistic character against alien oppressors. Henry Serruys has conclusively pointed out, however, that the facts controvert any such interpretation, since Chu Yüan-chang readily absorbed and made use of defecting Mongols and even ennobled Mongols who gave him meritorious service.[4] Such modern left-wing Chinese writers as Wu Han have charged, in angry disappointment, that Chu began as a champion of the people against alien oppressors but came to be manipulated and brainwashed by traditionalistic, "feudalistic," "landlord-class" Confucian advisers.[5] Although Chu was now ready to talk about "expelling the barbarian caitiffs and restoring China to the Chinese," the truth seems to be that, even to the end of his life, he felt a respect verging on awe toward the Mongols, as no doubt befitted anyone of his plebeian background.

Nevertheless, neither Chu Yüan-chang nor his marshals were afraid of the Yüan forces in the north after they had successively disposed of Ch'en Yu-liang and Chang Shih-ch'eng. They readily agreed not to delay action against the north until remaining resistance in the south had been destroyed, but to press northward at the same time as mop-up operations were conducted in the rear against Fang Kuo-chen in south coastal Chekiang and Yüan loyalists in the far south and southwest. There was some disagreement, though, about how to proceed against the Mongols. Chu's most flamboyant marshal, Ch'ang Yü-ch'un, who previously had to be restrained and reprimanded for acting too eagerly on his own initiative and for unnecessarily cruel treatment of the enemy, argued vigorously and repeatedly that an army sent directly against Peking could easily bring down the remnants of Yüan authority in one blow. Others were more cautious, and Chu himself argued that Shantung and Honan provinces must be occupied first, so that Peking could not expect reinforcements from these rear areas when it was finally assaulted. The campaign was planned accordingly, and it was carefully organized. Chu's lifelong crony Hsü Ta, proven a vigorous but disciplined and prudent general in every major campaign to date, was named overall generalissimo for the northern operations. Ch'ang Yü-ch'un was named vice commander in the understanding that he would lead the forward echelons. Among the subordinate commanders were Chu's nephew Li Wen-chung; Fu Yu-te 傅友德 , originally one of Ch'en Yu-liang's generals who had surrendered his army in 1361 and had subsequently fought well in Chu's cause; and Lan Yü 藍玉 , a Ting-yüan recruit who had been in Ch'ang Yü-ch'un's retinue since 1355. Chu lectured them all severely on the importance of maintaining discipline so that the armies would behave as trustworthy liberators of the people rather than as new oppressors. Specifically, soldiers were to be punished for the most common military excesses of the time--reckless killing, looting, damaging people's homes and personal property, killing plow oxen, and kidnapping.

Thus warned, and otherwise well prepared, Hsü Ta and Ch'ang Yü-ch'un were on the move northward through the Huai basin with a grand army of some 250 thousand men the month following Chang Shih-ch'eng's capitulation at Soochow late in 1367. In early spring of 1368, within three months, Hsü and Ch'ang had occupied the old Grand Canal and the surrounding lands up to the provincial capital of Shantung, Chinan. From there they moved westward up the Yellow River and captured Kaifeng, in Honan. Pressing on westward, they defeated a Yüan force outside Loyang. Then, joining a separate column that had been advancing northward through central Honan, they took possession of Loyang, the provincial capital, and regrouped to push on northward to Peking. In early summer Chu Yüan-chang personally came north to Kaifeng, where he convened his commanders and distributed praise and rewards. Kaifeng was named Northern Capital (Pei-ching) of the new dynasty.

Fortunately for the Ming forces, their advance to the north coincided with the peak of disorder among the Yüan forces. The heir apparent Ayushiridara and the Chinese-Mongol general Kökö Temür were struggling for control of the Yüan armies that were relied on to defend the capital, and regional commanders to the west, Li Ssu-ch'i and Chang Liang-pi, were antagonistic to both. Local Yüan garrisons in Shantung and Honan had proved too demoralized to offer more than token resistance. Many joined the Ming armies without resisting at all.

In late summer Hsü Ta and Ch'ang Yü-ch'un gathered their armies north of the Yellow River at Lin-ch'ing, Shantung, and raced to Peking by road and canal, virtually unopposed. Overwhelming a Yüan defense force at Ho-hsi-wu southeast of the capital, they occupied the principal suburban city, T'ung-chou, on September 9. The next night the Yüan emperor Shun-ti fled from Peking northwestward toward the steppe capital, Shang-tu. On September 14 Hsü Ta's army marched into Peking, and the Yüan dynasty was effectively at an end in China. The imperial prince regent Temür-buqa (T'ieh-mu-erh-pu-hua, or T'e-mu-erh-pu-ha) and his last defiant supporters were taken prisoner and promptly put to death. Bitter-end loyalists in the Yüan central government upheld the Chinese tradition of committing suicide in large numbers rather than submit to a new ruler; some native Chinese were among them. What remained of the Yüan imperial household staff, including concubines and eunuchs, were all shipped off to Nanking.

III. Organizing the New Dynasty

After formally taking the throne as first emperor of the Ming dynasty at the age of forty on the first day of the Chinese year 1368 (actually January 20, 1368, by Western reckoning), Chu Yüan-chang permitted few further references to his previous associations with the rebel Sung dynasty and the White Lotus and Red Turban movements that supported it. Giving his dynasty the name Ming ("brightness"), how-ever, linked him forever with these antecedents, and especially with the Manichaean tradition, in which the universe is conceived of as a battleground on which forces of light (good) and dark (evil) interminably contend. Since by 1367 Chu's court already considered Manichaean and other folk superstition doctrines unorthodox and disreputable, and since Chu himself soon developed obsessive sensitivities about this taint on his imperial respectability, the choice of such a dynastic name calls for some explanation. No explanation was offered at the time, however, and no fully satisfactory explanation has been offered by subsequent historians. One can only surmise that Chu's Confucian, traditionalistic advisers had not yet weaned him from the superstitions that had obviously pervaded his youthful thinking. That folk superstitions remained impor-tant even in Chu's adult thinking is amply demonstrated in his lifelong reliance, to an abnormal degree, on divination and other forms of prog-nostication for help in decision-making.[6]

Adoption of the dynastic name Ming is all the more puzzling be-cause in the normal pattern of past Chinese history Chu could have been expected to perpetuate the name Wu, having risen from the status of duke of Wu and then prince of Wu. The founders of past Chinese dynas-ties had normally used regional names of precisely this sort for their

new regimes, and Wu was a regional name of great historic distinction
that had not yet been used as the name of a major dynasty. In Chu
Yüan-chang's thinking, however, two considerations may have weighed
heavily against continued use of the name Wu. On one hand, Chang
Shih-ch'eng's use of the identical princely designation could only have
contaminated the name in Chu's mind after 1367, when Chang resisted
him with great vigor at Soochow and then arrogantly went to his death
without acknowledging Chu's legitimate overlordship. Moreover, Chu's
troubled early life in the harsh Huai basin must have made him self-
consciously and resentfully alien to the cultural elegance that characterized the Soochow heartland of the region traditionally most closely
associated with the name Wu. However ruefully he might have envied it,
the refinement conjured up by the name Wu was hardly in accord with
Chu's rude background, and he may have realized this with some dismay
in 1367.

Many traditions had been shattered, anyway. The Mongols had
followed a pattern of using ideological symbols, rather than regional
names, for dynastic names; Yüan (signifying "great," "primary") had
auspicious connotations of varied sorts. In breaking with the prior
Chinese tradition and following the Mongol pattern, Chu Yüan-chang
may have hoped that the Manichaean significance of the word Ming would
be overshadowed by the good connotations provided by the orthodox
Chinese tradition, in which Ming ("brightness") symbolizes the intelli-
gence and wisdom of esteemed rulers. The new dynastic-name pattern
endured, in any event, when the Manchus succeeded the Ming rulers in
the seventeenth century. Although the Manchus were early disposed to
use the dynastic name Chin, adopted by their Jurchen forebears in the
twelfth century, they came to the throne in China with the symbolic
dynastic name Ch'ing ("purity"), which was auspicious enough to match
Ming.

Chu Yüan-chang established another precedent by allowing the era-
name Hung-wu to extend unchanged throughout his reign. Previous
emperors had commonly used more than one era-name during the course
of their reigns, often changing them when circumstances suggested a
change of luck might be desirable. It was perhaps mere chance that
Chu Yüan-chang used only one, but his practice in this regard was
followed by all subsequent emperors, of both Ming and Ch'ing dynasties.
The era-names of these emperors, in consequence, have often been
used by historians as identifying names; for example, some writers
consistently refer to Chu Yüan-chang as the Hung-wu emperor, or even
simply as Hung-wu. Earlier emperors, in contrast, are consistently

referred to by their posthumous temple designations, as in the examples of Han Kao-tsu and T'ang T'ai-tsung. To avoid any possible confusion, Chu Yüan-chang will hereinafter also be referred to by his posthumous temple designation, T'ai-tsu ("Grand Progenitor"), and the term Hung-wu will be used only in reference to the era of his reign.

* * * * *

Capturing the Yüan capital was of course a climactic event symbolizing that T'ai-tsu had indeed displaced the Mongol Shun-ti as the legitimate ruler of China; but Mongol and other resistance groups remained in control of parts of the northwest, the far south, and the southwest. They had to be suppressed, and the expelled Mongols had to be kept at bay along the northern frontier. Moreover, an effective government had to be organized for the whole country, and administrative policies had to be established in every realm of government. Much of T'ai-tsu's thirty-year reign (1368-1398) was therefore devoted, of necessity, to these matters, laying the foundation for a continuing, stable regime.

Continuing Military Operations

Late in 1367, when Hsü Ta, Ch'ang Yü-ch'un, and others began their campaign in the north, T'ai-tsu organized other campaigns to quell remaining resistance in the south. For several years Fang Kuo-chen, on the Chekiang coast, had vacillated annoyingly, trying to appease the rising Ming power on his northwest while at the same time keeping in the good graces of the Yüan court far to the north. Now T'ai-tsu called for his complete surrender. Still he procrastinated. T'ang Ho was therefore delegated to destroy him. Coordinating his own coastal campaign with a drive across southern Chekiang from the interior, T'ang quickly brought such pressure to bear on Fang that Fang gave himself up before the end of 1367. He was taken captive to Nanking and was kept in honored custody there until his death in 1374.

Reinforced with Fang Kuo-chen's surrendered navy, T'ang Ho pressed on southward in combined sea and land operations and early in 1368 subjugated Yüan loyalist forces in Fukien province. While consolidating Ming control there, he detached a fleet that swept almost unopposed along the Kwangtung coast and into the far southern metropolis Canton. Simultaneously, a land and river force was pressing southward out of the central Yangtze region into northern Kwangsi, where Yüan loyalist resistance was crushed in a battle at Kweilin. By the end of summer in 1368 the whole southern region--Fukien, Kwangtung, and

Kwangsi--was firmly under Ming control. The aboriginal tribespeople of the far southwest, in modern Kweichow and Yunnan provinces, and the isolated Hsia state to the west in Szechwan posed no important threat to the empire and were left alone for later disposition.

* * * * *

When the Yüan emperor Shun-ti fled Peking in the autumn of 1368 there were still substantial, though uncoordinated, Yüan loyalist forces intact to the west, in Shansi and Shensi provinces. Kökö Temür was closest to Peking, and beyond him were the Chinese generals Li Ssu-ch'i and Chang Liang-pi. The Ming campaign plan called for these northwestern regions to be swept clear as soon as Peking had fallen, and Hsü Ta lost little time celebrating in Peking. He quickly moved into southern Shansi and skirmished with some of Kökö Temür's troops. But Kökö Temür had received orders from the fleeing Shun-ti to recapture Peking. No doubt thinking that, with Hsü Ta campaigning into Shansi, the imperial capital must be lightly defended, he evaded a confrontation with Hsü Ta and dashed toward Peking. Instead of falling back in a panic, Hsü Ta took advantage of Kökö Temür's maneuver eastward and drove straight on the Shansi provincial capital, T'ai-yüan. Kökö Temür wheeled about to defend his home base only to be met en route by the waiting Hsü Ta. Kökö Temür was totally routed and fled into the northwestern steppes. By the end of 1368 the whole of Shansi province was securely in Hsü Ta's hands.

Meanwhile the Yüan court at Shang-tu beyond the Great Wall had regained sufficient composure to send a large raiding party back into the Peking area. The Ming marshals Ch'ang Yü-ch'un and Li Wen-chung led an army of ninety thousand men out to drive the raiders off and then pursued them all the way beyond the Great Wall to Shang-tu itself. In the summer of 1369 they captured this Mongol headquarters, large numbers of surrendering Mongol chiefs and troops, ten thousand carts, thirty thousand horses, and fifty thousand cattle. Ch'ang Yü-ch'un died on this campaign and was genuinely mourned; but Mongol power in the Inner Mongolian region north of Peking had been dealt a ruinous blow. Shang-tu was turned into a Ming military outpost, renamed K'ai-p'ing; and Shun-ti fled farther out into the steppe, toward the ancient Mongol heartland in the Karakorum area north of the Gobi. Soon a Mongol raiding force retaliated by attacking Ta-t'ung on the frontier northwest of Peking, but Li Wen-chung drove it away.

While his associates were thus occupied in what might be called the central northern frontier zone, Hsü Ta pressed on westward in 1369.

The Yüan commander Li Ssu-ch'i fell back repeatedly before him and finally capitulated at Lin-t'ao, in modern Kansu province. Soon, while clearing away resistance elsewhere in China's far northwest, Hsü Ta defeated and captured Chang Liang-pi at Ch'ing-yang, in eastern Kansu. In 1370 Kökö Temür reappeared on the northwestern frontier, laying siege to Lan-chou in central Kansu. Rather than go directly to the relief of Lan-chou, Hsü Ta and Li Wen-chung mobilized to strike north toward the Gobi, whereupon Kökö Temür broke off his siege and rushed north to defend the Mongol homeland. Hsü and Li trapped and attacked him en route, but he escaped toward Karakorum.

By this time Shun-ti had established himself anew north of Peking, at Ying-ch'ang in modern Jehol province, but he died there in the late spring of 1370. His son Ayushiridara succeeded, but Ying-ch'ang was almost immediately attacked and ravaged by Li Wen-chung. The Yüan court was now thoroughly shattered. Ayushiridara's empress and his eldest son were taken captive and sent into honored custory in Nanking, along with great quantities of loot including the old imperial seals used in Sung and Yüan times. Yüan generals surrendered armies of thirty-seven thousand and sixteen thousand men. Ayushiridara and the remnants of his staff fled again into the western wastelands toward Karakorum. In the following year the Mongol commander at Liao-yang in the far northeast, which had not yet been directly threatened by the Ming armies, defected and peaceably brought modern Manchuria into the Ming empire.

In 1372 T'ai-tsu ordered a massive, three-column assault across the Gobi to crush Kökö Temür. Hsü Ta marched a Chinese army for the first time as far as Karakorum itself, on the Orkhon River at the far side of the vast Inner Asian wasteland. His exhausted army was defeated with thousands of casualties, but a supporting column under Li Wen-chung dispersed Kökö Temür's forces in sufficient disarray that they no longer posed a serious threat to the Chinese frontier. Kökö Temür's death in 1375 removed this particular threat entirely. The Yüan emperor Ayushiridara (d. 1378) and his son Toghus-temür (T'o-ku-ssu-t'ieh-mu-erh, d. 1388) remained active, however; and during the remaining 1370s and the 1380s the Ming generals Hsü Ta, Li Wen-chung, Lan Yü, Fu Yu-te, T'ang Ho, and others kept busy driving away raiders and establishing durable defenses. Li Wen-chung died in 1384, followed by Hsü Ta in 1385; and T'ang Ho retired in 1388. Lan Yü became the most active and successful marshal in the north in the 1380s.

Ming armies penetrated north of the Gobi again in 1380, under Mu Ying 沐英; and in 1387 Lan Yü was sent out to hunt down and destroy Toghus-temür. Crossing the Gobi once again, Chinese troops under his command occupied Karakorum in 1388 and pursued the Mongols on beyond, finally defeating them decisively near the far northern lake called Buir-nor. Toghus-temür's son was captured, but the Mongol emperor himself escaped only to be assassinated later in the year by one of his own followers. In 1390 T'ai-tsu again sent a great army northward, this time under the supervision of two imperial princes, and its sweep of the Inner Mongolian regions seems to have scattered remaining Mongol resistance there so thoroughly that the region could be considered securely under Ming control. Ming princes continued patrolling this section of the frontier, however, to the end of T'ai-tsu's reign in 1398.

In the far northeast, vigorous pacification efforts had also been required in 1387. The Liao valley, surrendered in 1371 but not really absorbed under Ming administration, was increasingly harassed from the north in the 1380s by a Mongol prince named Naghacu (Na-ha-ch'u, or Na-k'o-ch'u). In 1387 Lan Yü, Fu Yu-te, and others marched an army reportedly two hundred thousand strong up the narrow coast of the Yellow Sea into modern Manchuria and as far north as the Sungari River, where Naghacu finally surrendered in exchange for a noble title, after losing most of his supporters as defectors to the Ming. At least forty thousand Mongol captives were apparently welcomed and resettled with government subsidies; and a new Ming military stronghold was established at Ta-ning, in modern Jehol province.

All these campaigns against the Mongols in the Hung-wu period created an extensive Ming-controlled power zone outside the Great Wall that reached from Hami in modern Sinkiang (captured from Mongols in 1388) through modern Inner Mongolia south of the Gobi and eastward into the Liao valley of Manchuria. Kökö-temür in the far west, Yüan imperial forces in the central zone, and Naghacu in the far northeast had all been successfully subdued. Meanwhile, resistance on smaller scales in the newly conquered territories had also been systematically exterminated. Among the more interesting lesser figures in these activities was a virtually unidentifiable Yüan loyalist known only as "the Fourth Grand-prince" (Ssu-ta-wang 四大王), who led guerrilla fighters in the mountains of Shansi province from 1371 until 1388, when he was persuaded to surrender and was pardoned.[7]

* * * * *

By the time the Mongols in the north had been effectively suppressed--that is, by 1390--the Ming government had also brought under its control the modern provinces of Szechwan and Yunnan, where resistance had earlier been disregarded. Also, strenuous efforts were being made to subjugate all the aboriginal tribespeople of the southwest, in the hope that for the first time in history they might be assimilated into Chinese culture.

The Hsia regime in Szechwan, founded by Ming Yü-chen and subsequently allowed to deteriorate by his heir Ming Sheng and the military strongman Wu Yu-jen, was not a major problem. In 1371 a Yangtze River fleet commanded by T'ang Ho and an infantry force from Shensi to the north under Fu Yu-te converged on Hsia and overwhelmed it. Wu Yu-jen was killed, but Ming Sheng was taken captive to Nanking. He was kept there in honored custody along with the captured heir of Ch'en Yu-liang until 1372, when both were sent into exile in Korea.

The situation in Yunnan was somewhat more troublesome. Much of that remote and rugged region was under the control of the Mongol nobleman Pa-tsa-la-wa-erh-mi, known as the prince of Liang. T'ai-tsu repeatedly tried to persuade him to submit peaceably, using techniques that proved effective with most Yüan supporters in other areas, even those belonging to the Mongol imperial clan. But the prince of Liang was disdainful and even put envoys from T'ai-tsu to death in 1372 and 1375. In southern Yunnan there was, in addition, a long-established and defiant regime called Ta-li, representing one group of aboriginal tribespeople. Finally losing patience with his appeasement tactics, T'ai-tsu in 1381 organized an army reported to be three hundred thousand strong for a campaign to suppress all opposition in Yunnan. It was commanded by three generals with long experience on the northern frontier: Lan Yü, Fu Yu-te, and Mu Ying. By early 1382 they had completed their task. The prince of Liang, embattled, had committed suicide; Ta-li had collapsed; and the whole region was being organized in administrative units subordinate to Nanking. Mu Ying was left in charge as grand defender of Yunnan. After his death in 1392, the office was inherited successively by his descendants.

Few of the varied aborigines of southwestern China welcomed the intrusion of Chinese culture and control. Large groups of Ta-li aborigines had to be put down anew after 1382, with notable uprisings occurring especially in 1385 and 1388. Tribesmen of Hunan, Kwangsi, Kweichow, and Szechwan known as the Man peoples also rebelled repeatedly and were slaughtered in large numbers. A group of Shan tribesmen in the Lu-ch'uan area of the ill-defined border region between Yunnan and Burma troubled both China and the Ava kingdom in Burma throughout T'ai-tsu's reign, using Burmese elephants against Chinese forces and Chinese firearms against Burmese forces.

That T'ai-tsu retained his original era-name Hung-wu throughout his whole reign can possibly be explained by the fact that it seemed appropriate indefinitely; "vast military achievements" were indeed perennial. They constitute one of the major facets of the history of T'ai-tsu's time, and they were essential to the solidification of his new dynastic regime.

Creation of the Ming Government

Ming T'ai-tsu and his advisers at Nanking were busily occupied establishing an imperial government structure and formulating precedent-setting administrative policies while the generals were expanding and securing the frontiers. The creators of the new Ming government no doubt thought they were restoring the classic governmental patterns of the T'ang and Sung dynasties, and later historians have generally credited them with such a restoration. In fact, however, the Ming founder had little choice but to adapt the Yüan governmental apparatus that was ready at hand during the busy years of his rise to power. Thereafter, he gradually reshaped it into an unprecedented structure that was distinctively different from both its Yüan and T'ang-Sung antecedents.

The Yüan governmental structure under which T'ai-tsu came to manhood was in its own distinctive way a departure from the T'ang-Sung model. In the central administration the Yüan rulers had abandoned the classic tripartite division of responsibilities between a Chancellery, a Secretariat, and a Bureau of State Affairs. Instead, they consolidated general administrative functions in a unitary Secretariat dominated by two chief councilors or prime ministers, which directed a variety of subordinate agencies prominently including six functionally differen-tiated ministries. Local governmental responsibilities, as in earlier times, were delegated to prefectures (now appropriately called circuits, lu) and, subordinate to them, subprefectures and counties. Between the prefectures and the central administration at Peking, however, the Mongols introduced an intermediary level supervisory agency that might be thought of as a proto-provincial government, through which all prefectures except those close to Peking communicated indirectly with the central government. Originally, in the conquest period, these were mobile headquarters detachments of the metropolitan Secretariat, but gradually they settled into permanent agencies called Branch Secretariats, each with a named territorial jurisdiction. China was thus divided into ten large proto-provinces, as follows (the numbers of subordinate prefectures are indicated in parentheses):

1. the area directly administered from Peking, comprising modern Hopei, Shansi, Shantung, and Inner Mongolia (29 prefectures)
2. Liao-yang: modern Manchuria (7)
3. Shensi (4)
4. Kansu (7)
5. Honan: modern Honan and the northern parts of Hupei, Anhwei, and Kiangsu (12)
6. Szechwan (9)
7. Yunnan: incorporating part of modern Kweichow (37)
8. Hukuang: southern Hupei, Hunan, Kwangsi, and part of Kweichow (30)
9. Kiangsi: Kiangsi and Kwangtung (18)
10. Chiang-Che: southern Kiangsu, Chekiang, and Fukien (30)

Korea was at times considered an eleventh Yüan province, called Cheng-tung 征東 ; it had no subordinate prefectures.

Paralleling this general-administration hierarchy were two other hierarchies, of military and surveillance organs, with overlapping territorial jurisdictions. The military establishment was run by a unitary Bureau of Military Affairs at Peking, in liaison with the Secretariat's Ministry of War. In emergencies it set up field branches in the pattern of the early Branch Secretariats, but these were always ad hoc agencies and did not become permanent provincial-level military commands. The Branch Secretariats became accustomed to serving as the provincial-level coordinating agencies for the Bureau of Military Affairs as well as for the metropolitan Secretariat. Between the Branch Secretariats and the prefectures there were, however, some sixty relatively permanent army headquarters with many different kinds of names but generally called pacification commissions (hsüan-wei ssu) or regional military commands (tu yüan-shuai fu), some of which had subordinate local military commands (yüan-shuai fu). These exercised tactical control over prefectural-level military organizations that were literally called "commands of ten thousand" (wan-hu fu), and their constituent local garrisons.

The surveillance hierarchy maintained censorial watch over the activities of both civil and military personnel at all levels through a metropolitan Censorate at Peking, two Branch Censorates each responsible for several Branch Secretariats, and as many as twenty-four regional Surveillance Offices (su-cheng lien-fang ssu), each responsible for a designated group of prefectures and local military commands.

The basic skeleton of the Yüan governmental structure can perhaps be best suggested in diagrammatic form, as in figure 1, where straight lines indicate administrative control and arrows indicate surveillance jurisdiction.

Fig. 1. BASIC STRUCTURE OF YÜAN GOVERNMENT

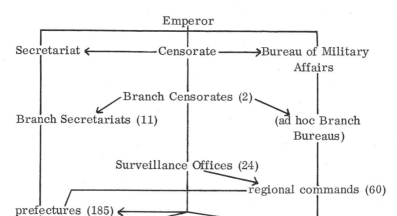

Ming T'ai-tsu as a young rebel had to accommodate himself to these existing governmental structures. When Kuo Tzu-hsing in 1352 seized Hao-chou, a subprefectural town, he called his headquarters a subregional military command in the Yüan fashion, that is, a yüan-shuai fu. When the Hao-chou rebels, including T'ai-tsu, spread their authority more extensively, Kuo Tzu-hsing came to be considered chief of a full regional military command (tu yüan-shuai fu); and it was this status that Kuo's son was given by Han Lin-erh in 1355, when T'ai-tsu had captured T'ai-p'ing on the south bank of the Yangtze. By then Han Lin-erh had set up a skeletal national government for his rebel Sung dynasty, with a Secretariat and a Bureau of Military Affairs in the Yüan pattern. Then in 1356, when T'ai-tsu captured Nanking, Han Lin-erh gave him nominal status in the Sung Bureau of Military Affairs and placed him in charge of a Chiang-nan ("from the Yangtze south") Branch Secretariat based at Nanking, with the title chief administrator (p'ing-chang). For a time the headquarters at T'ai-p'ing was considered a Branch Bureau of Military Affairs, and the new forward headquarters in Nanking had briefly been considered a regional military command subordinate to it. But the military headquarters at Nanking was quickly transformed into a Branch Bureau of Military Affairs, replacing the one at T'ai-p'ing. In 1359 T'ai-tsu was promoted to the status of chief councilor of the Chiang-nan Branch Secretariat. It should be noted, however, that the whole rebel Sung dynasty governmental structure was a thin facade in any event. T'ai-tsu, while paying proper homage to Han Lin-erh, was actually in total charge of the territories under his military control, and he delegated civil and military authority as he wished.

In the localities that came under his control in these early years, T'ai-tsu most commonly left the Yüan structure and personnel of civil government unchanged. He did consistently transform the Yüan prefectural designation lu ("circuit") into the more traditional designation fu, and occasionally he "demoted" a prefecture to the status of subprefecture or even county and "promoted" other units of local government. Such restructuring of the prestige ranks among towns and cities was not remarkable; it went on sporadically throughout Chinese history, and particularly during the founding of new dynasties. In general, T'ai-tsu's pattern was to establish a local military command (yüan-shuai fu) alongside each prefecture. In 1358, as the territory under his control expanded, he began setting up subbranch and then Branch Secretariats in the Yüan fashion, to coordinate the administration of groups of contiguous prefectures and military commands, each under a chief administrator (p'ing-chang).

At Nanking, under the most direct control of the Chiang-nan Branch Secretariat and the Chiang-nan Branch Bureau of Military Affairs, both of which T'ai-tsu personally administered, the city government had been organized as a prefecture called Ying-t'ien. Aside from some troops reserved as a personal bodyguard for himself, his armies were organized in five "wing" commands (i t'ung-chün yüan-shuai fu). When T'ai-tsu was given the honorific title duke of Wu in 1361, although he seems to have retained control of the Chiang-nan Branch Secretariat, he replaced the Chiang-nan Branch Bureau of Military Affairs with a new Chief Military Commission (ta tu-tu fu, another designation inherited from Yüan) and at least nominally relinquished his personal control in this realm to his nephew Chu Wen-cheng, named grand commissioner-in-chief (ta tu-tu).

In 1364, when T'ai-tsu assumed the title prince of Wu after having destroyed his western rival Ch'en Yu-liang, he reorganized his government into a structure that suggested greater independence and stability.

Having previously abolished the subordinate-sounding Branch Bureau of Military Affairs in favor of an independent-sounding Chief Military Commission, he now similarly changed the old Chiang-nan Branch Secretariat into an unqualified Secretariat; and he relinquished his personal status in it to two new chief councilors (temporarily called hsiang-kuo), the scholar Li Shan-ch'ang and the marshal Hsü Ta. At this time the Secretariat included four subordinate ministries, specializing in fiscal affairs, ritual affairs, justice, and construction. Simultaneously, basic military units under the Chief Military Commission were redesignated guards or garrisons (wei, a traditional designation also used to a limited extent by Yüan), thus presumably giving them a status less transitory-sounding than Yüan's local military commands (yüan-shuai fu) and less alien-sounding than Yüan's "commands of ten thousand" (wan-hu fu). The Yüan titles for lesser garrison officers, chiliarch (ch'ien-hu) and centurion (po-hu), were nevertheless perpetuated in the designations of the constituent battalions (ch'ien-hu so) and companies (po-hu so) of the newly designated guards. The Ming military garrison establishment retained this new structure thenceforth and was known by the general term "the wei-so system." Although it was given distinctive touches by Ming T'ai-tsu, it had evolved naturally out of its Yüan antecedent, as Romeyn Taylor has pointed out.[8]

This rudimentary governmental structure was greatly expanded and somewhat rearranged in 1367-1368, when T'ai-tsu made the final transition from regional warlord to emperor of a new dynasty, as his armies brought virtually all of China proper under his control. The Chief Military Commission was deprived of its solitary grand commissioner-in-chief in 1367, perhaps because T'ai-tsu did not care to think of a single subordinate having even nominal control over his fast-growing military establishment. Two commissioners-in-chief (tu-tu) now divided the responsibility, as responsibility in the Secretariat was theoretically divided between two chief councilors (in 1368 renamed ch'eng-hsiang). The Secretariat's subordinate ministries were now expanded to the full traditional complement of six: Ministries of Personnel, of Revenue, of Rites, of War, of Justice, and of Works. A Yüan-style Censorate, with two censors-in-chief, was established to complete the top level of the central government in 1382, when a host of lesser agencies was also created.

Some minor office-juggling occurred in 1367 when T'ai-tsu decreed that the Yüan practice of giving the right side precedence over the left side should be abandoned in favor of the opposite practice of the older Chinese tradition. In offices where there were dual appointees of the same rank, as in the case of the Secretariat's chief councilors, the senior was now designated "of the left" and the junior "of the right" rather than vice versa, as had been the case.

The number of Branch Secretariats quickly increased to twelve, more or less creating the modern provinces of Chekiang, Kiangsi, Fukien, Kwangtung, Kwangsi, Hukuang (combining modern Hupei and Hunan), Shantung, Honan, Peiping (modern Hopei), Shansi, Shensi (incorporating modern Kansu), and Szechwan. Yunnan (incorporating much of modern Kweichow) became a thirteenth province in 1382, after the suppression of the Mongol prince of Liang and the aboriginal Ta-li regime there.

In a significant departure from the Yüan model, T'ai-tsu established permanent military and surveillance agencies alongside each Branch Secretariat, in every province, so that there was a clear tripartite division of responsibility at the provincial level. At first, the military agencies were briefly called Branch Chief Military Commissions, but then they were redesignated Regional Military Commissions (tu wei chih-hui ssu; in 1375 altered to tu chih-hui ssu, commonly abbreviated to tu-ssu). The Regional Military Commissions numbered thirteen in early Hung-wu times, there being one in each province and an additional one in modern Manchuria called Liao-tung (for civil administration considered a part of Shantung province). Moreover, three Branch Regional Military Commissions were soon added, so that the northern frontier provinces Shansi and Shensi and the southeastern coastal province Fukien each had two commissions. In 1382, when Yunnan was incorporated as a province, both a Yunnan and a Kweichow Regional Military Commission were created in it.

The provincial-level surveillance agencies were apparently never thought of as Yüan-style Branch Censorates; they corresponded more nearly to Yüan's lower-level and more numerous regional Surveillance Offices. From their inauguration in 1367 they were designated Provincial Surveillance Offices (t'i-hsing an-ch'a ssu). There was close liaison between them and the Censorate at Nanking, but they were not directly subordinate to the Censorate in the way that Branch Secretariats were subordinate to the metropolitan Secretariat. Both the military and surveillance agencies at the provincial level had solitary commissioners in charge, unlike most of the capital agencies, which had dual administrators.

In 1376 the Branch Secretariats were all transformed into Provincial Administration Offices (ch'eng-hsüan pu-cheng ssu), each headed by two commissioners. This change was a reduction in the status and power of the former Branch Secretariats. The new agencies remained directly subordinate to the metropolitan Secretariat despite the autonomous ring of their new names, and their responsibilities were more narrowly defined. In general, as provincial-level government evolved in the ways described, it became clear that control over each province was being fragmented among three coequal agencies: one for general (especially fiscal) administration, one for censorial surveillance and judicial administration, and one in administrative charge of the province's military garrisons. The senior officials of the three agencies deliberated together about important matters, forming a collegial policy-formulating body. There was no provincial governor; the provincial government was this collectivity, commonly known as "the three offices" (san-ssu).

The overall early Ming governmental apparatus is illustrated in figure 2. Straight lines suggest administrative control; broken lines suggest closely cooperative relationships rather than supervisory control; and arrows suggest surveillance jurisdiction.

Fig. 2. EARLY MING GOVERNMENTAL STRUCTURE

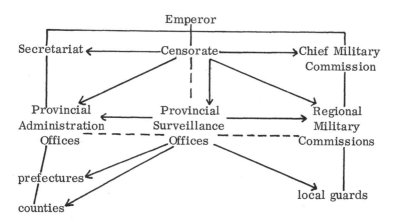

The large region around Nanking that T'ai-tsu considered his home base, comprising modern Kiangsu and Anhwei provinces, was made a metropolitan area administered directly from the capital. It was known as "the capital" area (ching-shih) or as "the Southern Capital" area (Nanking) or as "the directly-attached" area (chih-li). The Mongol capital at Peking was reduced to prefectural status and made capital of the Peiping province, which corresponded to the jurisdiction of the Yüan metropolitan Secretariat.

As both F. W. Mote and E. L. Farmer have emphasized, there was doubt for some time about where the Ming capital should finally be located.[9] Nanking was a comfortable and convenient place in that it had easy access to abundant agricultural resources and was a strategic point for both land and water transportation. Moreover, it had a certain majestic aura deriving from its long history as a regional capital. However, T'ai-tsu had no strong personal ties to it; it had never served as a national capital; and it was located far south of the North China Plain, which the Chinese had always considered the heartland of their nation and the logical site of their capital. In the early years of his reign, therefore, T'ai-tsu assumed that he would eventually establish a permanent capital somewhere in the north. As has already been noted, the ancient capital city Kaifeng, on the Yellow River, was given the honorific status of Northern Capital (Peking) after its capture in 1368, and T'ai-tsu visited it twice that year. But it apparently did not appeal to him, for it remained no more than the provincial capital of Honan, and no effort seems to have been made to construct imperial-scale buildings there. The honorific designation Peking was finally canceled in 1378. In the meantime, the prestige and advantages of such other ancient northern capitals as Loyang, also in Honan, and Changan (modern Sian), in Shensi, were repeatedly discussed at the Nanking court. And as late as 1391 T'ai-tsu sent his heir apparent to tour Shansi and Shensi, partly to evaluate possible sites for a new capital. The death of the heir apparent in 1392 from some illness contracted on this trip to the northwest may have seemed a warning from Heaven. By this time, too, the central government had substantial roots in Nanking. In the last years of his reign, in any event, T'ai-tsu spoke enthusiastically of Nanking's advantages as a national capital, pointing out its symbolic reflection of the southward shift in population and wealth that the nation had experienced in recent centuries.

T'ai-tsu's place of origin, the modern Feng-yang area in northern Anhwei, received special treatment. T'ai-tsu may even have considered making it the site of his national capital. In 1369 he gave it the honorific designation Middle Capital (Chung-tu), and in succeeding years he had imperial-style palaces built there in profusion, together with a shrine dedicated to his ancestors. Throughout his reign Feng-yang was used as a combination vacation resort and exercise ground for the imperial family. T'ai-tsu's younger sons and his grandsons were often sent there for tutoring in military skills.

* * * * *

The year 1380 has always been singled out by historians as the major turning point in the evolution of the structure and the style of government in Ming times, for early in that year T'ai-tsu "abolished" the whole upper echelon of his central government and concentrated power securely in his own hands. This significant change followed the dismissal, trial, and execution of the senior chief councilor Hu Wei-yung 胡惟庸, who was charged with plotting to overthrow T'ai-tsu and establish a new dynasty. Many other high-ranking officials were implicated and punished, and T'ai-tsu clearly concluded that the existing governmental structure made possible so much centralization of power in the hands of his ministers that his own authority was endangered. He consequently dismantled all of the government's top-level organs: the Secretariat, the Chief Military Commission, and the Censorate.

A tendency on T'ai-tsu's part to be jealous of power concentrations had long been evident. As has already been noted, the Chief Military Commission had been deprived of its solitary grand commissioner-in-chief in 1367, even though at that time real military power was fragmented among such field commanders as Hsü Ta. The downgrading of Branch Secretariats in 1376, when administrative control over provinces was divided among the three coequal agencies described above, might also be attributed to T'ai-tsu's fear of too-powerful appointees. It must also be kept in mind, however, that in these early years of T'ai-tsu's reign the territory under Ming control was expanding rapidly, governmental tasks were increasingly becoming more numerous and complex, and administrative units were consequently proliferating with great speed, both in the central government and at local levels. In 1373-1374, for example, the Secretariat's six ministries had each spawned from three to five subordinate, specialized bureaus in efforts to improve management of their burgeoning responsibilities. The tripartite division of provincial-level responsibilities in 1376 can perhaps be interpreted similarly, as acknowledgement that provincial government was becoming too complex for the solitary administrator of a Branch Secretariat to cope with efficiently. In many ways T'ai-tsu demonstrated that he was concerned with governmental efficiency as zealously as he was jealous of his imperial authority. His restructuring of the central government in 1380, however, resulted in the most inefficient structure conceivable, since it left him in the role of sole coordinator of twelve autonomous top-echelon administrative agencies, rather than three as before.

The dismantling of the Secretariat was the most prominent and most vengeful aspect of the 1380 reorganization. Not only the dual chief councilors, but all other executive officials of the Secretariat were deprived of their posts. What remained of the Secretariat was the group of formerly subordinate, coequal but now uncoordinated, six ministries, each with a solitary minister in charge. These now came directly under T'ai-tsu's personal supervision and were the new highest-level general-administration agencies in the empire. T'ai-tsu felt so vengeful that he decreed no Secretariat should ever again be established, and in succeeding years he repeatedly made pronouncements binding his heirs in perpetuity to impose the death penalty on anyone who dared propose reappointment of chief councilors.

Control over the empire's military establishment was simultaneously reorganized in a somewhat different fashion but with the same fragmenting effect, the former Chief Military Commission being multiplied into five coequal Chief Military Commissions. Differentiated by the designations Front, Rear, Left, Right, and Center, the new agencies were each given administrative control over a group of Regional Military Commissions in the provinces and a proportion of the guards that were stationed around the capital and not subordinate to Regional Military Commissions. None of the five Chief Military Commissions had a prescribed complement of commissioners-in-chief; the numbers varied from year to year in no fixed pattern. The generals appointed to these and to lesser executive offices in the five commissions were somewhat comparable in functions to a modern joint chiefs of staff, but the structure really made T'ai-tsu his own chief of staff, as well as his own prime minister. Moreover, the generals were rapidly losing their early predominance in governmental affairs as governance shifted from a military to a civil emphasis. The real burdens of administering, equipping, and supplying the empire-wide military establishment, both in garrisons and on campaigns, were falling more and more on the Ministry of Revenue, the Ministry of Works, and especially the Ministry of War. What administrative responsibilities were left to the five Chief Military Commissions is not yet wholly clear. By the end of T'ai-tsu's reign their executive officers constituted a pool of generals who were consulted about defense problems and were available for tactical assignments in command of forces on campaign, but had relatively little to do with the standing army in garrison status.

The reorganization of 1380 affected the surveillance hierarchy harshly, although the harshness was quickly moderated. For reasons that are not clear, all Provincial Surveillance Offices were even abolished; but, in 1381, they were all reconstituted. Abolition of the Censorate at the capital was a decapitation similar to that inflicted on the

Secretariat: the offices of censors-in-chief and vice censors-in-chief were swept away, and censorial responsibilities were delegated directly to numerous junior-rank investigating censors, grouped in a leaderless collectivity called the Court of Surveillance (ch'a-yüan). This chaotic condition was rectified in 1382, when the investigating censors were organized into twelve new agencies called Circuits (tao) named after the contemporaneous provinces, and a chief investigating censor was appointed in each. (This made the emperor sole coordinator of twenty-three upper-echelon agencies: five chief military commissions, six general-administration ministries, and twelve censorial circuits.) Then in 1383 a new executive superstructure was imposed on the Circuits, comprising three grades of censors-in-chief; and the reunified censorial agency was given the new name Chief Surveillance Office (tu ch'a-yüan). The Censorate was thus the only top-echelon agency to be restored as a unified entity. However, its reunification was largely superficial; its functions remained as effectively fragmented as were those of the other previous executive organs of government. Censors-in-chief no longer exercised, as in the case of the Yüan Censorate, centralized direction of all surveillance activities. They were superiors of the investigating censors for purposes of personnel administration within the organization, but in maintaining censorial surveillance over the officialdom at large the investigating censors were individually and directly responsible to the throne.

After 1380, in short, Ming government was structured so that no single appointee could possibly gain overall control of either the military, the general-administration, or the surveillance establishment. Executive control was kept in the hands of the emperor, and the burden was enormous. In one ten-day period late in T'ai-tsu's reign, 1,660 documents dealing with 3,391 separate matters are reported to have been presented for imperial decision.[10] T'ai-tsu quickly realized that he could not cope with such multitudinous problems entirely by himself. Even before the end of 1380 he created a high-ranking advisory staff called the four grand counselors (ssu fu-kuan) outside the regular chain of administrative authority; and in 1382 this staff was superseded by a newly established group of four (later five) special palace attendants called grand secretaries (ta hsüeh-shih), whose nominal function was to tutor the heir apparent but who became the emperor's confidential advisers in general. Even so, it must be considered that T'ai-tsu personally ran his government to the end of his reign. But the central government structure he had created, by demanding such vigorous and detailed supervision on the emperor's part, could hardly have been perpetuated unchanged by less diligent successors; and it did change further, as will be noted below.

T'ai-tsu's Administrative Policies

While the great early Ming marshals were subjugating the empire militarily and T'ai-tsu and his advisers were setting up a governmental structure through which to administer it, major administrative policies were simultaneously being formulated, tested, and reformulated. Decisions reached in this period came to be esteemed subsequently as a kind of unconsolidated dynastic constitution; and its prestige grew as time passed, although T'ai-tsu's successors were not rigidly reluctant to modify it.

T'ai-tsu was thus busy, and he was also conscientious. As his modern biographer Wu Han has emphasized,[11] he disliked the complexities and obfuscations that government clerks are commonly fond of. He wanted people to know what was expected of them, and he wanted this stated in simple and direct language. Probably no dynastic founder in Chinese history more assiduously prepared, promulgated, and publicized the rules and regulations that he wanted obeyed. First in the torrent of such publications that issued from his government was the rudimentary, one-volume Ming Law Code (Ta Ming ling 大明令) of 1368, which underwent several revisions thereafter and achieved final form, in 460 articles, in 1397 (entitled Ta Ming lü 大明律). In 1368 and 1369 there appeared codified regulations governing the conduct of palace women and palace eunuchs, in both cases warning vehemently against irregular intrusions into government business by palace personnel. A Surveillance Manual (Hsien-kang shih-lei 憲綱事類) appeared in 1371 as a guide for censorial officials. In 1373 came a Daily Register (Jih-li 日曆), a compilation of what might be called policy decisions made since the beginning of T'ai-tsu's rise to power; and the first edition of Ancestral Instructions (Huang Ming tsu-hsün 皇明祖訓), compilation of which had begun in 1369 and which was to be revised in 1376, again in 1381, and finally in 1395. This latter work was T'ai-tsu's effort to provide a basic policy guide for his posterity. It lays heavy stress on rules of personal conduct for members of the imperial family. A Guide to Funerals and Mourning Practices (Hsiao-tz'u lu 孝慈錄) followed in 1374, and 1375 brought Comprehensive Instructions about Public Responsibilities (Tzu-shih t'ung-hsün 資世通訓) addressed both to the officialdom and to the people at large. One of the most important and revealing works of T'ai-tsu's whole reign, the Imperial Commandments (Yü-chih ta-kao 御製大誥), was published in installments from 1385 to 1387. This is a record of important criminal cases with the emperor's personal commentaries, which vividly point out the dread fates that awaited malefactors.

Thereafter came Prescribed Ritual Proceedings (Li-i ting-shih 禮儀
定式, 1387), Central Government Functions (Chu-ssu chih-chang 諸
司職章, 1393), Regulations for the Nobility (Chi-ku ting-chih 稽古
定制, 1396), Regulations for Schools (Hsüeh-hsiao ko-shih 學校格
式, 1397), and finally On Educating the People (Chiao-min pang-wen
教民榜文 1398), a preachment on the Confucian moral principles
that the common people were exhorted to practice.

T'ai-tsu's diligence is also reflected in the extent to which he
made himself accessible to officials. He instituted a schedule of three
general audiences daily--at daybreak, noon, and sunset--at all of which,
apparently, all officials stationed in the capital were expected to be
present. So exhausting a court regimen was probably unprecedented in
Chinese history, and none of T'ai-tsu's successors maintained it. As
the modern historian Ch'ien Mu has exclaimed, "This can be called
real diligence in administration!"[12] T'ai-tsu also regularly summoned
local officials from all parts of the empire to audience at the capital.
There was a first great convocation of local-government officials at
Nanking in 1368, at which T'ai-tsu lectured them about his philosophy
of government; and it was subsequently arranged that local officials
should regularly come to imperial audience at three-year intervals.
Although this practice persisted throughout the dynasty, many such
audiences in later reigns were mere formalities conducted in the emperor's absence, and it is likely that no later emperor in any way gave
such personal attention to local-government personnel as T'ai-tsu did.

* * * * *

Personnel. One of the most important problems that T'ai-tsu
faced during his rise to power, of course, was how to find and properly
utilize men who could be trusted to command his armies and administer
his government. The problem was especially difficult because, unlike
almost all other founding emperors in Chinese history, T'ai-tsu had no
personal or family connections in the existing government when he began
his career; he had no personnel resources, among either relatives or
family clients, comparable to those normally available to the scion of
a traditional "great family." Moreover, the Yüan officialdom was largely
alien, antagonistic, or suspect; and the scholar class in general was not
favorably disposed toward, or trusted by, populist rebels. T'ai-tsu's
success in creating a new ruling class virtually out of nothing suggests
great pragmatic wisdom on his part and, as Romeyn Taylor has pointed
out, "that the institutions and principles of imperial government, far
from being the peculiar property of a ruling elite or the distinguishing
marks of a 'great tradition', were part of the common heritage of the
Chinese people."[13]

T'ai-tsu sought and welcomed trustworthy supporters wherever he could find them: among the original Huai basin Red Turban rebels, among defecting militia leaders and village chiefs of the Yüan establishment, among ambitious young adventurers who were ready to flock around any promising leader, among defectors from rival rebel chieftains along the Yangtze, among surrendering rivals of every sort, and even, as his prestige grew, among the originally disdainful educated classes of southeastern China. T'ai-tsu had little choice in the early years but to hope for the best from whatever talents were at hand, since there was no time for systematic recruiting. Thus his staff grew haphazardly during the 1350s and 1360s, with newcomers of various backgrounds being co-opted for service with each new expansion of territorial control.

It is noteworthy--and it was natural under the circumstances-- that personal loyalty to himself, tested over many years, was the real touchstone of success in T'ai-tsu's service. Though he had to accept support whenever it was offered during his rise to power, and though he respected and rewarded demonstrated competence on anyone's part, latecomers to his service were seldom given top-level responsibilities until he was solidly entrenched on the throne. No one ever surpassed T'ai-tsu's boyhood friend Hsü Ta in favor and honor. All 4 of the men who served as chief councilors and 5 of the 6 who served as censors-in-chief before all such offices were abolished in 1380 had come into T'ai-tsu's service not later than 1355; and of the 104 men who were awarded elite noble titles during the entirety of the Hung-wu period, 71 had joined him not later than 1360.[14] On becoming emperor, T'ai-tsu repeatedly spoke rather apologetically about his regime's being dominated by men from his native region, and especially from Fengyang.

Once the Ming empire was consolidated, systematic arrangements naturally had to be made so that a constant flow of new men came into service, to supplement and eventually succeed the staff members of the conquest era. To this end, a National University was established at Nanking in 1368 for the purpose of training sons of officials and other promising young men for careers in government. The next year, acting on the principle that "the primary thing in governance is transformation through education, and schools are fundamental to transformation through education," T'ai-tsu ordered that schools be established in all prefectures, subprefectures, and counties, each with a state-supported teaching staff and state-subsidized students. Detailed regulations about school administration were issued in 1382 and, as has already been noted, were published in final form in 1397. It was also ordered that schools be set up in all of the empire's military garrisons. In 1375 T'ai-tsu even began urging provincial and local governments to foster the opening of community-supported elementary schools in all villages. It is clear that by the end of T'ai-tsu's reign a substantial beginning had been made toward creation of an unprecedented empire-wide system of publicly supported, though by no means universal, education. The prescribed curriculum at every level emphasized the ancient Confucian classics, Ming laws, and T'ai-tsu's Imperial Commandments.

T'ai-tsu used the local schools to feed educated young men systematically into his officialdom. In 1383 he set forth a procedure by which promising students in the local state schools should regularly be promoted into the National University, as so-called "tribute students" (kung-sheng), to be prepared there for subsequent official appointments. He thus opened a wide channel into the National University, and National University graduates had prominent governmental careers in the early Ming reigns. T'ai-tsu often appointed National University students directly to highly responsible offices; in 1389 one student was catapulted into the post of assistant censor-in-chief.

T'ai-tsu seems to have had a very special fondness for the National University students, apparently thinking them idealistically pliable and thus preferable for certain tasks to established officials. As early as 1369 he dispatched a large group of students on general inspection trips throughout the empire. In 1375 a group of 366 students was sent out to oversee the establishment of local schools in North China. In 1387 National University students made a monumental cadastral survey of the rich Yangtze delta prefectures, on the basis of which new tax registers were prepared. In 1391 a group of 639 students was sent out to audit records in all provincial and local government offices, and in 1394 another large contingent was scattered throughout the empire to initiate and foster irrigation and other waterways-construction projects.

Another device that T'ai-tsu used extensively to bring new men into his service was the traditional one of recommendations. Throughout his rise to power he relied on Li Shan-ch'ang and other scholar-advisers to seek out and recruit promising new administrators, and his generals were ever ready to promote meritorious soldiers into positions of leadership. When T'ai-tsu established an imperial-style central government of his own at Nanking in 1364, he ordered his new Secretariat to see to it that all local units of government annually presented men of talent to be considered for suitable appointments, either civil or military. In 1367 and again in 1368 he sent special agents out into the provinces to recruit talented men who might have been overlooked by the local authorities and to persuade those who might be reluctant to serve. In 1370 and 1373 he issued special proclamations emphasizing the government's need for new talents and calling on all officials then in service to intensify their recruitment efforts. It was even specified that talented old men aged sixty or more should not be overlooked; they could be given honored retiree status, and used as counselors, in the Hanlin Academy, a pool of litterateurs in the capital that was regularly used for compiling imperial publications. The vigorous talent search of the Hung-wu era was highly productive. There were recommendees who were appointed directly to such responsible posts as vice censor-in-chief, grand secretary, provincial administration commissioner, and vice minister; and several recommendees eventually rose to the eminent positions of ministers in the six ministries. For decades after T'ai-tsu's reign, men who had been recruited in this fashion in his time were prominent in the central government.

Direct recruitment of personnel through schools and recommendations was of much greater importance in Hung-wu than in subsequent Ming eras. Even though both avenues into the officialdom remained technically open and respectable to the end of the dynasty, in practice recruitment through recommendations was discontinued early in the fifteenth century and recruitment through schools was of virtually no significance after the middle of the fifteenth century. Both systems were eventually superseded in practice by recruitment through competitive public examinations, a revival of the dominant Sung dynasty practice. The examination system was institutionalized in T'ai-tsu's reign, but not without hesitance on T'ai-tsu's part.

Since recruitment examinations, in the view of the educated classes, were essential to any regime claiming imperial legitimacy, it was natural that in 1367 T'ai-tsu should order his Secretariat to prepare for the inauguration of an examination system. Early the next year it was announced that preliminary examinations should be conducted in provincial capitals (and at Nanking for candidates of the metropolitan area) in the eighth month to provide qualified candidates for a first triennial metropolitan examination to be held early in 1371. These examinations were conducted on schedule, producing 120 metropolitan degree-holders commonly called doctors (chin-shih). Before the next series of scheduled examinations could be held, however, T'ai-tsu in early 1373 ordered that recruitment through examinations be temporarily suspended. This occasioned one of his proclamations exhorting local officials to intensify their recruitment of personnel through recommendations. T'ai-tsu's reason for suspending the examinations was his disappointment with the quality of the new civil servants produced in 1371. They were, for his taste, too bookish and immature. "We sincerely sought worthies," he complained to the Secretariat, "and the empire responded with empty phrase-makers. This is by no means what we intended." In ordering an intensified resort to recruitment by recommendations, he insisted that "virtuous conduct must be primary; literary skill is secondary."[15]

In 1382 T'ai-tsu was prevailed upon to order resumption of the traditional recruitment examinations at three-year intervals, and the second series was conducted in 1384-85. Meanwhile, early in 1384, T'ai-tsu promulgated regulations to govern the examination procedures. Local educational officials would certify both students and non-enrolled scholars who were qualified to take the provincial examinations, and the examinations would consist of three sessions spanning a week. There would be one session devoted to interpretation of passages from the ancient Confucian classics, one devoted to exercises in the writing of official documentary styles, and a third devoted to essays applying classical and historical precedents to generalized governmental problems. As in Yüan times, examinees were required to adhere to the classical commentaries of the Chu Hsi school of Sung Neo-Confucianism. The metropolitan examination was to be similarly organized, in three sessions. Passers of the metropolitan examinations would subsequently take a one-session palace examination, nominally presided over by the emperor himself, devoted to a single question relating to current problems, on the basis of which they were to be ranked in a final order of excellence. Such was the examination system practiced throughout the remainder of the dynasty. It soon became the preeminent avenue by which educated young men entered the civil service, and after the early Ming decades few men reached positions of influence in the civil administration without having won examination degrees.

In any examinations of such sorts men from the wealthy and cultured southern provinces had a significant advantage over northerners, and active discrimination was charged in 1397, when the fifty-one men who passed the doctoral examination included not a single northerner. Northerners who failed petitioned T'ai-tsu for reconsideration. Himself a northerner, T'ai-tsu angrily appointed a new board of examiners to check the examination papers. Sixty-one names were consequently added to the pass list, and the original examiners were punished. A

precedent had been established that would soon lead to the assignment of
rigid pass quotas according to a regional division of China so that south-
erners, and espcially southeasterners, could not exploit their natural
advantages to the point of monopolizing the civil service.

For other personnel needs of the government, T'ai-tsu followed
the Yüan practice of requiring service on a hereditary basis. As a
matter of fact, it would not be erroneous to consider the whole population to have been classified into hereditary categories in early Ming
times as well as in Yüan times, the categories clarifying the nature of
the individual's obligations to the government. There were, of course,
official families whose status was achieved by the non-hereditary procedures described above; but as soon as a new official had demonstrated
competence in his first appointment, his father and grandfather were
entitled to retroactive honorific appointments; and when an official
attained relatively high rank, it was provided that one or more sons
could automatically become eligible for appointment to specified lesser
posts. The agrarian masses and others of non-specialized occupations
were classified as civilian families and were expected to bear the heav-
iest burden of taxes and intermittent corvée services. Families that
worked at special crafts were registered in various categories of artisan
families and were expected, theoretically in perpetuity, to provide
craftsmen for necessary government work. In T'ai-tsu's reign more
than two hundred thousand artisan families, chiefly with skills in construction work, were permanently resettled in Nanking as a government-
paid skilled-labor force. Other registered artisan families were left
in their homes to pursue their livings independently, but they were
required to send one worker each to Nanking for a short period of government work at intervals of from one to five years. Workers in the
government-monopolized salt manufactories scattered about the empire
were also registered hereditarily and were dealt with in much the same
fashion as were those artisans who were permanently resident at the
capital.

The most prominent and most publicized aspect of the Ming
hereditary-registration practice is the wei-so system of military garrisons that has already been referred to, which constituted the Ming
standing army. Those officers and soldiers who were originally in
T'ai-tsu's service went into the census registers as a self-perpetuating
military class distinct from civilian families and the various artisan
families. When new territories were conquered, the local residents
were generally allowed to choose individually whether to be registered
as military or as civilian families. The surrendering armies of

T'ai-tsu's rivals were normally registered en masse as military families. Many categories of criminals were also subject to reclassification into hereditary military status. In the late years of T'ai-tsu's reign, when China proper was almost entirely consolidated and stabilized, military families probably accounted for about two million of the ten million registered families of all sorts that were reported in the national census. In other words, the registered national population of some sixty-five million persons included perhaps two million men on hereditary duty in the standing army.

The general principle was that whenever an officer or a soldier died or otherwise became unavailable for service his family was obligated to provide a suitable adult male to take his place. Because of this obligation, military families were excused from some of the tax and corvée burdens borne by civilian families. This standing army was eventually supplemented by draftees from local militia units that all magistrates were called upon to organize among the civilian and artisan families of their jurisdictions. Some such local militia units came to have highly specialized military skills; Fukien men were traditionally China's best sailors, for example. Other militia groups won great fighting renown. Miners from various localities were notoriously tough fighters, and several Buddhist monasteries could be counted on regularly to provide highly skilled fighters.

Among the fighting forces that were highly esteemed and often relied on in emergencies were the frontier peoples not yet assimilated into Chinese culture. Mongol, Turkic, and proto-Manchu tribespeople along the northern borders who accepted Ming overlordship were used as an outer-defense buffer between China proper and the hostile "barbarians" beyond them. For the most part, they were allowed to carry on their traditional ways of life in their traditional homelands under chieftains of their own choosing, usually hereditary. But they were nominally incorporated into the standing army in the wei-so pattern, their chieftains being automatically confirmed as military officers with appropriate Chinese titles. Aboriginal tribesmen of the southwest were handled somewhat differently. Although they were similarly allowed to live their traditional lives so long as they were peaceable, and although they were also generally governed by their hereditary tribal chieftains, they were nominally incorporated into the Chinese civil administration rather than into the military establishment. They were thus organized into prefectures and counties; and among them were supervisory units of special types, in the Yüan fashion called Pacification Commissions (hsüan-wei ssu and similar designations). Chinese of both civil and military services were commonly on the staffs of the aboriginal chieftains, although this was not the practice in the north. Many aboriginal tribesmen were feared fighters, and they were regularly summoned to service on campaigns both against other aborigines and in distant regions of China.

It should be noted that merit was not wholly disregarded in the military service. Only garrison-level posts were hereditary. Appointments in the Regional Military Commissions in the provinces and the Chief Military Commissions in the capital, as well as tactical commands of every sort, were not subject to inheritance but were given to officers of demonstrated merit for tenure at the emperor's pleasure; they retained their original garrison-level posts for inheritance purposes. It was also apparently anticipated, when T'ai-tsu in 1367 first ordered plans to be formulated for an examination system, that open competitive examinations would be used to recruit new military officers as well as new civil officials. Nevertheless, the heredity-recruitment system seems to have worked well enough in practice. Military examinations were not conducted in T'ai-tsu's time, and even after they were instituted belatedly in 1478, the examination passers never had the importance in the military service that their counterparts enjoyed in the civil service.

Persons who served T'ai-tsu with extraordinary loyalty and distinction were rewarded with status in a feudal-sounding nobility that in fact had few genuinely feudal characteristics. The nobility naturally included T'ai-tsu's twenty-six sons and sixteen daughters, designated imperial princes and princesses. Provisions were also made for their consorts and heirs, in perpetuity though in most instances with steadily decreasing ranks generation after generation. These members of the imperial clan were all given state stipends and were forbidden to enter the civil service or engage in labor or trade. T'ai-tsu apparently did not foresee what consequences this policy was to have. New imperial princes and princesses, and their offspring, were added to the original complement in each new reign, and by the end of the Ming dynasty the number of imperial clansmen who were on the state payroll and forbidden to participate in productive occupations has been estimated to have grown beyond one hundred thousand.

Officials and officers who served with special merit were ennobled with ancient titles normally translated, in order of ranks, as duke, marquis, earl, baron, and viscount; the latter two ranks were discontinued early and were not revived by T'ai-tsu's successors. Some dukes, marquises, and earls were authorized to transmit their noble status hereditarily, and some were not. All were allocated generous state stipends. None, however, had any legal territorial rights deriving from his noble status. Neither did they have prescribed duties except when called upon to give counsel or render special service, most often in command of troops on campaign. T'ai-tsu ennobled some of his civil officials, but for the most part--and solely under his successors-- awards of nobility were made to generals. It became the practice for distinguished civil officials to be given honorific noble titles posthumously, without any inheritance rights.

Because of these various limitations imposed by T'ai-tsu on the status of the nobility, nobles per se never became a significant group in the Ming administration. Noble status was no more than a titular honor, carrying special monetary benefits, conferred upon eminent members of the officialdom, almost always generals.

* * * * *

Particular precautions were required for the imperial household establishment. In the Chinese tradition an imperial household could only be staffed by women and eunuchs, and both palace women and eunuchs had recurringly throughout Chinese history taken advantage of their intimacy with emperors to exercise irregular influences on government--influences that moralistic officials and historians had consistently considered baneful. T'ai-tsu was at first generously inclined to treat the women of his household and their relatives with great honor; but his empress, the orphaned Miss Ma whom he had married at the beginning of his career as a rebel, persuaded him to heed the lessons of history in this regard. He therefore made it official Ming policy that imperial relatives by marriage should not be ennobled and, further, should not be allowed to take any role in government. Moreover, he made it the practice that imperial princes (hence emperors-to-be) take consorts and concubines from the families of relatively low-ranking military officers. His dynasty was thus saved from the troubles that several previous dynasties had experienced with powerful imperial in-laws. T'ai-tsu also prescribed that the staff of palace serving women be small, not exceeding a total of ninety-three persons distributed among units that were given specified responsibilities: for regalia, for clothing, for food, for the imperial bedchamber, and so on. T'ai-tsu reportedly told the Secretariat, "Although empresses and concubines are patterns of motherhood to the whole empire, they must not be permitted to take part in administrative matters; and lesser female attendants should be no more numerous than needed to provide service and to attend with towels and combs."[16]

T'ai-tsu was even more stern in his attitude toward palace eunuchs. He repeatedly lectured his advisers about the historic growth of the eunuch system and its threat to governmental stability. He insisted that eunuchs be kept both few and illiterate, and in 1384 he installed in the palace a cast-iron plaque bearing the warning, "Eunuchs must not interfere in governmental business. Violators will be beheaded." On one occasion he angrily expelled from the palace an aged eunuch with a long record of excellent service simply because he was overheard, in a casual way, referring to some matter of state. The ideal eunuch in T'ai-tsu's view seems to have been one "who knew his place and could be intimate without being arrogant. On encountering an official, he bowed and withdrew without opening his mouth." As early as 1375, nevertheless, T'ai-tsu began violating his own stern prohibitions by sending eunuchs out into the provinces on special assignments; and already in his reign there were objections from officials that there were too many eunuchs. On the whole, however, T'ai-tsu seems to have prevented eunuch abuses that had characterized some previous dynasties and were to become, as the modern scholars Ting I and R. B. Crawford have emphasized, sensationally excessive in later Ming reigns.[17]

Domestic administration. T'ai-tsu's policies in the socioeconomic realms of domestic administration, and their subsequent modifications and effects, cannot be discussed in detail here. Giving them brief attention is essential, however, to an understanding of the complex problems that T'ai-tsu faced on assuming the responsibilities, in the traditional Chinese term, of being "father and mother of the people," of the intricate social engineering that was resorted to in coping with these problems, and of the style or tone of governance that T'ai-tsu thereby bequeathed to his successors. Three kinds of problems were uppermost in his mind and deserve particular attention: (1) stabilization of the disrupted social order, (2) restoration of economic productivity and creation of an equitable method of providing for the state's fiscal needs, and (3) provision of logistical support for the defense establishment in the strategic but underproductive north.

Chinese society had been changing markedly since T'ang times, and the century-long Mongol occupation of China had brought severe social dislocations. The north, ravaged by successive wars and with its irrigation systems neglected, was underpopulated and agitated with heretical ideologies such as those in whose cause T'ai-tsu himself had become a rebel. In the south, and especially the populous and productive southeast, gross social inequities had been imposed by large landlords and rich merchants on the agrarian masses, many of whom had been reduced to the status of migrant workers or even slaves. Moreover, strong loyalties to such rival rebels as Chang Shih-ch'eng were to be expected in recently subjugated areas, and people everywhere had grown accustomed to mistrusting any central government and to recognizing local and regional interests exclusively.

One of T'ai-tsu's first acts aimed at restoring social stability was to abolish all forms of slavery. Then he utilized various precedents from Sung and earlier times to formulate a social organization system called li-chia (later pao-chia), by which the whole population was subdivided into communities (li, later pao) that were comparable in some ways to modern wards or precincts. The system evolved slowly through the Hung-wu years until it attained essentially final form in 1381, and the community unit seems to have worked with reasonable efficiency as an agency both of local self-government and of ideological and social control on the part of the state. The system was applicable to all elements in the population, whether rural or urban, and even to China's numerous boat-dwelling families of the southern provinces. Each community in theory consisted of 110 neighboring households. Heads of the 10 most prosperous households, as determined by the county magistrate or his agent, were designated community chiefs and served annual tours in rotation as representatives of the community in dealings with the county magistrate or, in tax matters, with intermediary tax collectors. The remaining 100 households were subdivided into ten tithings (chia) of 10 households each. In each tithing 1 household provided a tithing chief to represent his tithing to the community chief.

Each community functioned in accordance with a so-called community agreement, a sort of constitution for local self-government prepared by the members in a pattern prescribed by imperial edict. This agreement provided for the communal management of all local affairs and especially for the settling of disputes by the community chief; for the magistrates chastened communities that could not resolve their own intra-community litigations. The community agreement also included an exhortation to all citizens, prescribed by T'ai-tsu, that they should be filial and obedient to their parents, be respectful to their superiors, be harmonious within the community, educate their sons and brothers, be content each in his lot, and not do evil. The entire text of the agreement was read aloud at monthly community assemblies, and participants in the assemblies also recited an oath that they would preserve propriety and the law, would not permit coercion of the weak, would deal with lawlessness themselves within the community, would care for the poor, and would assist one another to bear the burdensome expenses of weddings and funerals. The community was expected to maintain a community altar for religious ceremonies, a community school, and a community granary for charitable uses.

Through the community organization the government requisitioned corvée labor services from the people as needed for work on large-scale construction projects on roads and waterways, irrigation systems, public buildings, and the like; to provide lictors, couriers, transport bearers, and menials of various other sorts for the county governmental establishment; and eventually for local militia service. Also, each community as a whole was a guarantor of the good conduct of all its members, and it could be held responsible for derelictions in adjacent communities.[18]

Once having turned his back on his own early loyalties as a Buddhist monk and a Red Turban rebel and having become a champion of orthodox Neo-Confucianism, T'ai-tsu adopted special measures to keep unorthodox religious groups under control. Secret society-like religious activities were banned entirely, and there was no official tolerance for Yüan-espoused Lamaism. Other Buddhist sects as well as Taoism were officially tolerated, and some religious were individually treated with great honor. The hereditary Taoist patriarch Chang Cheng-ch'ang 張正常 (1335-1378) of Kiangsi province was installed in Nanking and spent most of his last years there under government patronage. T'ai-tsu personally showed great favor to the successive Buddhist patriarchs Pandita Sahajasri (Pan-ti-ta Sa-ho-tsan-shih-li 班的達 薩曷拶室哩 d. 1381) and Tsung-lo 宗泐 (1318-1391); he sent the latter on a mission to Tibet and India spanning the years 1378-1381 in search of lost Buddhist sutras, and in 1379 he published new commentaries by Tsung-lo on several Buddhist canons. T'ai-tsu was also not niggardly in supporting the construction of new Buddhist temples at Nanking and elsewhere. Moreover, in 1382 he assigned Buddhist counselors to each of his princes, specifically to take charge of continuing devotions for the lately deceased Empress Ma. Despite all this, T'ai-tsu established restrictions on the religious orders that checked religious influence on government so effectively that the Ming period was probably less troubled by religiously inspired disturbances than any other of the imperial era.

This pacification of the religious orders was accomplished principally by their incorporation into the state government apparatus. Patriarchs of the two orders were appointed nominal heads of a Central Buddhist Registry and a Central Taoist Registry at the capital, and the leaders of local religious establishments were named to comparable offices at the prefectural, subprefectural, and county levels. All were supervised by the Ministry of Rites, and the religious leaders were held accountable to the ministry for the activities of their orders. They were required regularly to examine all monks, to issue government certificates to those who qualified, and to dismiss from the orders all those who were not genuine practitioners of the doctrines. Other controls were also attempted, although in practice they were probably unenforceable. The size of religious communities was severely restricted. The number of either Buddhist or Taoist monks and nuns in any one county, for example, was limited by law to twenty. A further restriction prevented the orders from recruiting monks before the age of forty and nuns before the age of fifty.

T'ai-tsu not only kept people under control; he moved them about in large numbers. In 1370 he issued a special invitation for landless families of the populous southern regions to move northward into uninhabited areas and reclaim them. It was provided that oxen, seed, and farm tools would be given such new settlers by the government and that they would be exempt from land taxes for three or more years. In that year alone he had more than 4,000 landless families moved out of the Yangtze delta into the Feng-yang region, and in 1371 a total of 140,000 Yangtze delta families, including some well-to-do farmers who had no wish to move, were reportedly induced to follow. In 1382 more than 24,000 persons from Kwangtung were moved into reclamation settlements elsewhere in northern Anhwei; in 1388 landless farmers of bleak Shansi province were moved in large numbers onto the more promising plains of Hopei and Honan; and in 1390 another large contingent of Yangtze delta farmers was moved into the Huai basin. Criminals were offered pardons if they became colonists in land-reclamation centers, and large numbers of them apparently accepted this kind of rehabilitation. By such policies, T'ai-tsu provided stable livelihoods for countless impoverished families, brought thousands of uncultivated acres under production, and reduced population pressures in the southeast.

Resettling people at the capital was also a significant social policy of T'ai-tsu's time. As has already been noted, craft-skilled families from all over the empire were brought into Nanking to serve as a resident corps of artisans needed by the government. The capital also had a large contingent of military garrisons, which is said to have numbered 200,000 individuals by 1390. But T'ai-tsu wanted to glorify his capital as well as to guard and staff it, so he regularly ordered large numbers of wealthy families to take up residence there. On one occasion he reportedly summoned 14,300 rich families from all parts of the empire to new Nanking homes; and in 1381 he required some 45,000 rich families of Soochow and other Yangtze delta cities formerly under Chang Shih-ch'eng's control to move to the capital. Their adult males were often assigned to corvée labor on palace-construction projects, for the mass summonses of rich families from the southeast were to some degree seen as punishments of potential dissidents as well as efforts to make Nanking more affluent and refined.

T'ai-tsu's policies concerning reclamation of unworked land were of course an essential part of his efforts to restore and invigorate the national economy. Confiscation and redistribution of the Yüan dynasty's government-owned lands and the estates of Yüan-favored large landlords also contributed to stabilization of the agricultural order. As in the cases of other dynastic founders, T'ai-tsu undertook extensive water-works construction projects in all areas; and he repeatedly canceled or reduced land taxes in areas that had been drained for long years to support his rise to power and in other areas that suffered from severe natural calamities. Economic rehabilitation in the north was facilitated by the continuing spread of sorghum, which had been introduced to China in Yüan times, as a supplement to the traditional dry-field crops, wheat and millet.

T'ai-tsu clearly intended to equalize land-tax burdens as best he could, taking into account the great variations in quality and productivity of soil from one locality to another. The monumental cadastral survey made in 1387 was probably China's most effective effort up to that time to establish a complete and accurate land register for tax purposes. The land taxes that T'ai-tsu imposed were relatively low. Ray Huang has even argued that they were unrealistically and unnecessarily low, with the unfortunate consequence that revenues were insufficient for national needs in later reigns.[19] A notable exception was made in the case of the Yangtze delta area taken from Chang Shih-ch'eng, where taxes were kept at an extraordinarily high rate. The classically punitive case is that of Soochow prefecture, which, with only one eighty-eighth of the taxable land in the empire, paid approximately one tenth of the empire's total land taxes. Soochow in combination with its neighboring prefectures of Sung-chiang and Ch'ang-chou paid more land taxes than any whole province. In 1380 T'ai-tsu relented and reduced the tax levels in this richly productive area, but they still remained by far the highest rates in the country.

Textile production was fostered by T'ai-tsu's order of 1368 (even though it was rescinded in 1395) that one-half mou of land on even the smallest farm, and at least a full mou on larger farms, must be planted in mulberry, hemp, or cotton. Taxes in kind were imposed, except that taxes on mulberry-leaf yields were deferred until trees were three years old. Farmers who failed to comply were required to pay taxes in finished cloth at punitive rates. China as a whole benefited from the fact that cotton, which had become widespread only in Yüan times, was now becoming a valuable national product. Cotton wadding was especially useful as quilting material for military uniforms and other clothing in the north. Great textile manufactories, both state-owned and private, came into existence at Nanking, Hangchow, and Soochow. During the Hung-wu period, also, salt production was restored under state monopoly. Salt was distributed in compulsory sales by the state directly to individual families, but the family quota was small enough that traders thrived on private retail sales of salt purchased wholesale from the government.

T'ai-tsu seems, on the whole, to have promoted a more favorable atmosphere for trade than had prevailed in either Yüan or Sung times. Mercantile taxes were both few and relatively low, and merchant families were not significantly discriminated against in the social order. Nonetheless, private business was by no means free of government controls. T'ai-tsu provided that government inspectors should regularly check on the accuracy of scales and measures in mercantile establishments, and keep records of commodity prices. Anyone whose goods were of less than acceptable quantity and quality or whose prices were deemed exorbitant was subject to punishment by the government.

Merchants and craftsmen customarily organized themselves into local guilds according to the types of commodities or services with which they dealt, and the guilds largely determined the conditions of trade in their spheres. Each had a guild chief certified by the government and held responsible by the government for the conduct of the guildsmen. Boat traders were similarly organized under harbor chiefs. Traders could travel about only with passports issued by the government, and every guild chief and harbor chief was required to present to the government each month a complete accounting of the identities and activities of all visiting traders. In order to prevent too complete monopolization of trade by resident guild chiefs, T'ai-tsu established in some cities government-operated trading warehouses, from which merchants might sell directly to retail outlets.[20]

The Yüan paper money had long been discredited and unused when T'ai-tsu established his new dynasty in 1368. Following the traditional custom, he issued copper coins in several denominations. By 1374 the market economy was recovering to such an extent, however, that there was a major shortage of coins. In response to requests from the mercantile community, T'ai-tsu in 1375 began issuing new paper money. Private ownership of gold and silver was forbidden; all supplies were ordered turned in to the government. The new paper money was not convertible, and its value steadily declined. T'ai-tsu successively ordered that certain categories of taxes be collected partly in paper money and that certain kinds of government payments be made in paper money, in efforts to maintain the currency in use. In 1393 he even temporarily forbade the circulation of copper coins; but by the end of his reign it was apparent that paper money was doomed. Bulk silver, in spite of government restrictions, was rapidly becoming the standard monetary unit in the markets, as it remained throughout the dynasty. Silver had even become a standard item of government tax income, beginning not later than 1376.

The Ming state revenue, as Ray Huang has shown, was necessarily a patchwork of many sorts of receivables, partly in money but mostly in kind. There were specific tax rates based either on the proprietary unit (for example, one mou of farm land) or the consumption unit (for example, mercantile goods taxed on an ad valorem basis), but the tax rates were not necessarily uniform throughout the country. Moreover, they were manipulated at the local level so as to produce collection quotas that were imposed on the county and regional government agencies. The national land-tax revenue target set by T'ai-tsu was approximately 29.5 million piculs of grain or its equivalent. Although T'ai-tsu intended that collection quotas should be adjusted periodically to reflect changed population and productivity patterns, his quotas actually became an almost unchangeable fixed ceiling on land-tax revenues for the rest of the dynasty.

Many kinds of taxes were collected directly by government agencies responsible either to the central government or to local government units. For collection of the land taxes, however, T'ai-tsu in 1371 set forth a procedure making the people themselves responsible for collection. Subcounty tax-collection districts were established everywhere, each district comprising an arbitrarily delimited aggregation of lands the tax revenues from which amounted to a uniform unit of ten thousand piculs of grain. The head of one prosperous family within each district was designated by the county magistrate as tax

captain (liang-chang), and all the tax captains in one county served as
fiscal intermediaries between the magistrate and the farming population.
Each tax captain was required to deliver his tax quota to a designated
government granary, normally in two installments per year, called the
summer tax and the autumn tax.

Since T'ai-tsu's capital at Nanking was located in the heart of
China's most productive agricultural region, and easily accessible by
cheap water transport, this tax-collecting and -delivering system served
both local and national needs quite well during his reign. But there was
one important exception. That is, despite the substantial efforts already
described to resettle people and restore agricultural production in the
north, the tax-captain system could not provide adequately for the needs
of the huge armies that T'ai-tsu kept òn duty along the northern frontier.
The fact that China's agricultural surplus was to be found in the south
whereas the need for that surplus was predominantly in the north made
a logistical problem that was of great gravity throughout the Ming period.
Eventually the problem was to be resolved by an elaborate restoration
of the deteriorated Yüan-time Grand Canal; but T'ai-tsu solved it for
his time by three other techniques.

1. Following the late Yüan practice, T'ai-tsu had tax grain trans-
   ported by sea from coastal depots in the southeast around the
   Shantung peninsula, bound not for the Peking area but for armies
   stationed in modern Manchuria. The navy that had been surrendered
   by the coastal rebel Fang Kuo-chen was principally relied on, as in
   late Yüan times, for this transport work. But the work was very
   hazardous because the transport convoys were highly vulnerable to
   storms, and every year losses were high. In 1374 one convoy lost
   forty ships, more than seven hundred men, and more than one-
   third of its cargo in a storm. T'ai-tsu himself reportedly said,
   "When a worker's family hear that he has to go to sea to transport the annual grain rations of the troops they believe that they
   have said goodbye to him forever."[21] The people directly involved
   dreaded the work, and the system was only partly satisfactory from
   the government's point of view. Nevertheless, sea transport persisted to the end of T'ai-tsu's reign.

2. In hopes of making the frontier forces as nearly as possible self-
   supporting, T'ai-tsu repeatedly ordered the extension in the north
   and northwest of the military-colonies system that he had adopted
   for his rebel forces as early as 1358. Garrison forces were
   assigned government lands on which, in a rotational pattern,

soldiers were delegated to do farming chores during intervals between active guard and patrol assignments. As late as 1388 the emperor was still ordering all his military garrisons to develop such agricultural supports. In productive lands such as those of modern Manchuria there was indeed a realistic prospect that garrisons could provide their own food; but prospects were bleak in the barren or marginal lands along the general line of the Great Wall, stretching from northeast of Peking to far western Kansu. For the large armies stationed in such areas some supplementary farming was possible, and in the Hung-wu era these potentialities were exploited probably more fully than in any later reign. But even a combination of military-colony production and deliveries of tax grains from the underpopulated and underproductive nearby provinces was sufficient to provide no more than the barest minimum logistical support.

3. The problem of feeding the northern and northwestern frontier forces was satisfactorily resolved for T'ai-tsu's time by one of the more ingenious bureaucratic schemes concocted in his court. Promulgated in 1370, the system was called k'ai-chung 開 中 . It required merchants who wanted government-monopolized salt, on which they were accustomed to make substantial profits, to earn vouchers entitling them to salt by delivering grain to the northern garrisons. The system worked, primarily because interested merchants were ingenious enough themselves to develop large-scale "merchant colonies" in cultivable wastelands near the borders, where tenant farmers produced the grain necessary to provision the frontier forces and to get salt vouchers for their merchant landlords. The system actually had the beneficial side effects of helping to resettle and promote general economic recovery in the north.

T'ai-tsu liked to boast of having created a military establishment that imposed no fiscal burden whatever on the civilian population, which is of course an exaggerated claim. Nevertheless, his measures aimed at alleviating that burden seem to have served their intended purposes effectively. In general, his domestic administration policies taken all together created a remarkably stable society and facilitated substantial economic growth by the end of his long reign in 1398.

Foreign relations and defense. Social stability and economic prosperity in the Hung-wu era resulted in part from T'ai-tsu's reluctance to undertake military adventures beyond China's frontiers. It was enough, in T'ai-tsu's view, for the Chinese to expel the Mongols and secure their traditional borders; and it was only prudent under the circumstances for the state to conserve its remaining resources for socioeconomic rehabilitation. Such was the predominant traditional attitude of Chinese governments, in any event, and T'ai-tsu was fond of repeating traditional axioms in this vein, such as: "As to the control of the barbarians of the four quarters, we have only to be militarily prepared and to attend to our frontier defenses. Resist them when they invade us but do not pursue them relentlessly when they withdraw."[22] Except for his determined efforts to keep the Mongols of the north and northwest on the defensive, T'ai-tsu was not aggressive toward neighboring peoples.

T'ai-tsu did have opportunities to engage in military meddling afar. During his reign there were dynastic upheavals in neighboring Korea and Annam (modern North Vietnam) that might have provoked a more adventuresome emperor to intervene forcibly, but T'ai-tsu accepted the results of these local power struggles with equanimity. In the late years of his reign he watched with some anxiety as an expansive new Mongol empire arose around distant Samarkand under Tamerlane, but T'ai-tsu did nothing militarily even when Tamerlane put to death two of his envoys to Samarkand.

T'ai-tsu was nevertheless aroused to action against two foreign peoples. In one case, the Turkic-Mongol rulers of Turfan, in modern Sinkiang in China's far west, annoyed him by harassing tributary caravans moving along the ancient oasis trail of Central Asia, and in 1377 he dispatched an army to destroy them and bring their area under direct Chinese supervision. The other case was more troublesome, involving coastal raiders based in southern Japan known most commonly by the Japanese term Wakō (Wo-k'ou 倭寇). Japanese coastal raiding, uncontrollable at the source because of extended political disunity in contemporaneous Japan, became a nuisance in Yüan times, and as early as 1369 Wakō flouted the new Ming imperium by raiding Shantung province. The raids continued, adding a new menace to the naturally hazardous sea transport of grain to the north. In 1370 and 1380 T'ai-tsu sent harsh messages threatening to undertake a punitive military campaign against Japan if they did not stop, but there was apparently no serious intention even to consider such strong measures. T'ai-tsu contented himself with keeping coastal defense forces as strong and alert as possible. In 1374 one Chinese coast guard fleet pursued a large Wakō squadron to the Ryukyus and there destroyed it; and between 1384 and 1387 the great marshal T'ang Ho undertook to make the Chekiang and

Fukien coasts secure. He supervised the building of fifty-nine fortified walls in the Hangchow region that were in active use as late as the 1550s, and he organized a special defense force of fifty-eight thousand soldiers to man them.

In general, T'ai-tsu chose to play the traditional Chinese emperor's role of tolerant and paternalistic overlord of neighboring "barbarians." In a speech on foreign affairs to his court officials in 1371 T'ai-tsu stated what would become the dynastic policy: "As for the little barbarian states beyond our frontiers, over the mountains and across the sea, located in far corners [of the world], it is my view that if they do not menace China we should not invade them." In the Ancestral Instructions that were promulgated in final form in 1395 he warned his successors "not to rely on the wealth and power of China to seek the temporary glory of war or to wage wars without good cause."[23] The Ancestral Instructions specifically listed fifteen states that China ought never invade, notably including Japan, Korea, the Ryukyus, modern Taiwan, Annam, Champa (modern South Vietnam), Cambodia, and Thailand. What T'ai-tsu expected of these states, and more distant peoples of the south and west, was respectful tributary relations of the traditional sort. He entrusted the supervision of such foreign relations to the Ministry of Rites and agencies subordinate to it, including Maritime Trade Superintendencies (shih-po ssu) at Ningpo in Chekiang for reception of envoys from Japan, at Ch'üan-chou in Fukien for dealings with the Ryukyus and Taiwan, and at Canton for relations with the states of Southeast Asia. Foreign relations, however, were supposed to be limited to officially sanctioned tributary activities. T'ai-tsu explicitly forbade any Chinese to go beyond the borders except on official government business, partly to prevent renegade Chinese from assisting real or potential enemies and partly to keep the Chinese uncontaminated by foreign cultures.

As has already been emphasized, T'ai-tsu was willing even to be tolerant of those Mongols in the north who would cooperate; but maintaining strong defenses along the northern frontier was nevertheless the major principle of Ming dynasty foreign policy. It was clearly not enough to have large numbers of wei-so forces in garrisons strung along the frontier; they had to be organized for tactical operations as well as for mere military administration. To this end, T'ai-tsu began organizing what eventually came to be called the nine frontiers (pien 邊) or nine defense areas (chen 鎮)--large zones of tactical-command responsibilities that stretched across North China from Liao-tung in modern Manchuria to Kansu in the far west. The basic defense-area line included the following:

1. Liao-tung
2. Chi-chou 薊州, the zone northeast of modern Peking
3. Hsüan-fu 宣府, the zone directly northwest of modern Peking
4. Ta-t'ung 大同, the northernmost portion of Shansi province
(Hsüan-fu and Ta-t'ung are commonly referred to jointly by the abbreviation Hsüan-Ta)
5. Yen-sui 延綏, the northeasternmost portion of Shensi province
6. Kansu, then referring to the northwestern part of modern Shensi province, and
7. Ning-hsia, then referring to the northeastern part of modern Kansu province.

In 1369, when the extramural Yüan capital Shang-tu was captured from the Mongols, it was transformed into a Ming stronghold called K'ai-p'ing; and in 1387, when the northeastern Mongol raider Naghacu was defeated, another extramural Ming stronghold was created at Ta-ning in modern Jehol province. To the end of T'ai-tsu's reign these two far northern outposts dominated what might be considered two additional defense areas, but both were subsequently abandoned. The eighth and ninth of the later Ming "nine frontiers" came into being thereafter, one at P'ien-t'ou 偏頭 pass in northernmost Shansi province and one at Ku-yüan 固原, far south of the Great Wall in the eastern part of modern Kansu province. Ku-yüan was not really a separate defense area; it was a headquarters supervising the three westernmost defense areas: Yen-sui, Kansu, and Ning-hsia.

The defense areas were not identical with provinces or with the territorial jurisdictions of Regional Military Commissions. They were somewhat fluid tactical commands superimposed upon the military-administration network--commands to which officers and men under the administrative control of nearby Regional Military Commissions were assigned as needed for active campaigning or for active guard and patrol duty at posts along the Great Wall and beyond. Peacetime guard and patrol duty was normally rotational. The men in charge of the troops on such tactical duty were normally nobles holding appointments in the Chief Military Commissions at the capital. They were given ad hoc designations as generals-in-chief (ta chiang-chün) or generals (chiang-chün) when on large-scale campaigns, or as regional commanders (tsung-ping kuan) or grand defenders (chen-shou) when on routine defense assignments. In each defense area there were various subordinate tactical officers, on more or less temporary duty detached from their hereditary wei-so posts in the regular military-administration hierarchy. Most provinces also came to have regional commanders who were similarly responsible for the tactical utilization of garrison forces in their provinces.

The Quality of T'ai-tsu's Reign

That T'ai-tsu rose from the commonest status in society to the throne, expelled the Mongols, and during a long reign stabilized Chinese government and society in patterns that would endure into modern times makes him one of the unchallengeably great figures of Chinese history. In the normal course of events it could be expected that the Chinese would revere him as the founder of a major dynasty; and indeed his successors on the throne, both of his own and even to some extent of the succeeding Ch'ing dynasty, cited many of his acts as wise and honored precedents from which they dared not depart. At the same time, however, T'ai-tsu is one of the most desecrated rulers of Chinese history. Most modern scholars would agree with F. W. Mote's contentions that T'ai-tsu was "the cruelest and most vicious tyrant of all Chinese history," perhaps mad, and creator of "a ruthless and vicious despotism"[24] that has had regrettable influence on all subsequent governance in China.

Modern left-wing and communist writers in China have debated vigorously and at length about T'ai-tsu's place in the history of China's class struggles. The noted biographer Wu Han, himself a controversial victim of the Cultural Revolution of the 1960s, has pictured T'ai-tsu as an early champion of a people's revolution who on attaining success betrayed the revolution and restored the traditional social order dominated by the landlord-gentry class.[25] Wu Han's opponents claim that T'ai-tsu never favored the poor but sided entirely with the repressive, reactionary landlord class whose support was the sine qua non of his rise to power.[26] Non-communist scholars have not exercised themselves along these lines, taking it almost for granted that T'ai-tsu, beginning as an unsophisticated champion of the poor, found it pragmatically necessary to create a government of a more or less traditional sort in which the educated, landowning elite inevitably played a predominant role. What they deplore is the extent to which T'ai-tsu centralized governmental power in his own hands and intimidated those who served him.

The controversies about T'ai-tsu that have emerged among modern communist historians seem principally to be rhetorical exercises that have great relevance to modern Chinese history but contribute relatively little to a balanced understanding of T'ai-tsu and his times. To be sure, T'ai-tsu uprooted and resettled poor and rich people alike from one locality to another, in accord with his conception of the national need; imposed rigid social and ideological controls upon all; was not as generous as some other emperors in remitting taxes and pardoning crimes; and gave substantial social and economic privileges to the members of his new government, in the traditional fashion. He was apparently never enamored of the vague populism that was fanatically espoused by some Red Turban leaders; and there is no evidence whatsoever that T'ai-tsu at any time considered establishing anything resembling a people's republic. In his time the common people's lot, although not as abased as in Yüan times, was by no means substantially transformed from its perennial harshness; but T'ai-tsu was always conscious of his own impoverished background and sympathetic toward the difficulties of life among the poor, and he opened opportunities to commoners like himself that made his reign probably the high point of greatest vertical social mobility in China's history. Moreover, T'ai-tsu's favorite targets of vilification and punishment were the rich and the influential, of whom he was always prepared to expect the worst; and, except for personal disloyalty and disobedience, nothing roused him to anger more than their wronging the common people. Unlike the effusions of rulers with no experience of the common people's world, T'ai-tsu's repeated and fervent protestations about the imperative need to protect the common people from abuses and exploitation have an unmistakeable ring of sincerity.

From an early time, and especially after taking the throne, T'ai-tsu showed great distrust of those to whom he had to delegate authority which enabled them conceivably to abuse the people and to threaten his own power. As has been shown above, he regularly rearranged his early governmental structure so as to put himself ever more directly in control of affairs. Only after the so-called "abolition" of the Secretariat, the Chief Military Commission, and the Censorate in 1380, when provincial-level authority had already been fragmented, was he apparently satisfied that no one else could accumulate too much power. He was willing to pay the cost: bearing a very heavy burden of responsibility himself.

Important as this governmental restructuring was, it was merely symptomatic of a new tone that suffused the whole emperor-official relationship in T'ai-tsu's time. He might have no choice but to rely on others to administer the complex business of his empire; but he determinedly kept them in what he considered their proper places. Perhaps as never before--certainly not since the ancient era of Ch'in Shih-huang-ti if then--officials were made to feel they were no more than servants

of the emperor and were totally at his mercy. The low status of officials
vis-a-vis the throne was symbolized in T'ai-tsu's prescriptions for court
rituals. Whereas in earlier times officials addressing the emperor in
audience were allowed to sit or at worst stand, T'ai-tsu towered over
his court from a high dais and required that officials address him only
from kneeling positions.

Even though the extensive censorial establishment provided a
regular and pervasive channel for surveillance over the conduct of
officials, T'ai-tsu shamelessly employed private spies to report on
officials' misdeeds of the most private sort--or to invent them if T'ai-
tsu was determined to find fault. He also used his personal bodyguard,
the Embroidered-uniform Guard (chin-i wei), as a supralegal secret
service organization to make arrests, to torture, and to punish without
any governmental hindrance; and it focused its attentions almost exclusively on the officialdom. T'ai-tsu challenged, modified, and reversed
any official's decisions as he pleased, and he punished officials on any
pretext at any time in any fashion. Without any semblance of due process,
he demoted or fined them, "removed them from the register" and thus
deprived them of status and privileges as state-recognized literati,
exiled them to serve as common soldiers at the frontier, imprisoned
and tortured them, or put them to death. He legitimized cruel punishments that had previously been utilized only rarely and as acknowledged
irregularities.[27] Most commonly, T'ai-tsu subjected his officials to
humiliating beatings in open court whenever he took offense at them.
These so-called "court beatings" (t'ing-chang廷杖) of officials, which
were sometimes fatal, were not wholly unprecedented in Chinese history,
but T'ai-tsu resorted to such humiliations regularly, on an entirely
unprecedented scale. One contemporaneous source reports that officials of the capital always bade their wives and children farewell on
leaving for court audience each morning, and if evening came without
disaster they congratulated one another on surviving another day.[28]

There were four climactic cases in which T'ai-tsu's cruelty
toward the official class reached astonishing levels. The first of these
was the so-called "blank reports case" (k'ung-yin an 空印案) of 1376.
All government offices at the provincial, prefectural, and county levels
were required to submit annual fiscal reports to the Ministry of Revenue.
As would be normal in any bureaucratic system, experience proved that
accurate final reckonings often could not be made until local records
had been compared with counterpart records in the ministry. It had
therefore become customary for provincial and local officials to seal
and certify reports in which figures were omitted, to be completed only

when the report-delivering underlings could review drafts with ministry officials. When T'ai-tsu learned of this practice he condemned it as flagrant disobedience and dishonesty. He ordered that all responsible officials at all levels who had engaged in it be put to death and that clerical underlings be exiled to serve in the frontier armies. Tradition has it that more than ten thousand persons were punished, either because they were implicated in the "blank reports" practice or because they protested against T'ai-tsu's reaction to it.

The most famous case, which precipitated the great restructuring of the central government of 1380, centered upon Hu Wei-yung, then senior chief councilor. Hu was a Ting-yüan man who had joined T'ai-tsu in 1355 and had served in a variety of local and provincial offices before being summoned to a middle-level capital post in 1367. In 1370 he was promoted into the Secretariat, and in 1373 he became chief councilor. T'ai-tsu trusted, esteemed, and favored him; and he successfully aroused T'ai-tsu's resentment against any possible rivals, even including the marshal Hsü Ta. Eventually, according to all extant records (which are not necessarily unchallengeable), Hu developed his own imperial ambitions and connived with many men whom T'ai-tsu had chastised to carry out a palace coup. It is alleged that he even sent agents seeking support from the Mongols and the Japanese. All these plans remained secret from T'ai-tsu until Hu's son, falling from a horse, was run over and killed by a cart on a Nanking street, whereupon Hu murdered the cart driver. T'ai-tsu angrily ordered Hu to idemnify the victim's family, and Hu responded by calling on his out-of-town supporters to rise and take Nanking. The whole scheme was finally exposed to T'ai-tsu by a palace eunuch. T'ai-tsu after some hesitation had Hu and his closest associates put to death at the beginning of 1380. Investigation of the case continued through the following decade, and those who died as accomplices are reported finally to have numbered more than thirty thousand, including more than twenty noblemen.

The third great case, arising in 1385, had as its principal culprit the vice minister of revenue Kuo Huan 郭桓. T'ai-tsu accused him of having organized or condoned empire-wide racketeering that had drained as much as one-fourth of total state revenues for the year into private pockets. Seven million piculs of grain were collected from all over the empire as stolen government goods, and more than ten thousand persons were reportedly put to death for corruption, including the minister of rites and the minister of justice.

The last of T'ai-tsu's four great purges, in 1393, was perhaps his cruelest. The principal focus was the marshal Lan Yü, who had come into T'ai-tsu's service in 1355 and in the late 1380s had become one of his foremost active marshals. Lan had fought courageously and victoriously on all the northern fronts and in the conquest of Yunnan, and he had been ennobled as a duke with hereditary privileges. But he had crude soldierly habits, and T'ai-tsu had to reprimand him on several occasions. He once broke down a gate in the Great Wall and killed its guards when they did not promptly admit him on his return from a frontier patrol. It was rumored that he had ravished a captured Yüan imperial concubine and caused her to commit suicide in shame. He coercively consolidated lands of neighboring small farmers into his own estate. His arrogance embarrassed and increasingly irritated T'ai-tsu, perhaps especially after Lan warned the heir apparent that the prince of Yen, T'ai-tsu's fourth and favorite son, was taking on imperial airs at his palace in modern Peking. In 1393 an officer of the Embroidered-uniform Guard denounced Lan for plotting a rebellion. After an apparently hasty investigation T'ai-tsu accepted a guilty verdict and had Lan put to death. A list of fifteen thousand men who were reportedly implicated in the planned rebellion was promulgated, and all were ordered executed. They included one duke, thirteen marquises, two earls, and civil officials as well as military officers, most notably the minister of personnel and a vice minister of revenue.

The middle years of T'ai-tsu's reign witnessed many more such purges on a lesser scale and countless instances of vicious punishments of individuals. T'ai-tsu particularly suspected the literati class of ridiculing him in puns, which come easily in Chinese because of its abundance of homophones. He had contemporaneous writings searched for anything that might be construed as veiled derision, especially any referring to his inelegant background; and the use of words (and there are many) that sounded like "monk," "shaven pate," or "bandit" in contexts where they could be interpreted as indirect disparagement of the emperor put one in mortal danger. It is often suggested that the full tide of T'ai-tsu's paranoid punishments of his enemies, real or imagined, was unleashed with the death of the astute Empress Ma in 1382. The empress had unquestionably been a stabilizing influence on T'ai-tsu throughout his rise to the throne, and he had relied on her heavily for counsel. Her passing no doubt removed a restraint on his more brutish urges, and it may have precipitated irrational fears by making him feel sorrowfully isolated and defenseless.

In his last years T'ai-tsu seems to have felt some remorse and become less brutal. In 1387 he reined in the feared Embroidered-uniform Guard, ordering all its torture instruments destroyed and its prisoners transferred to the regular judicial agencies; and in 1393 he issued detailed prohibitions against the Guard's customary methods of arresting, torturing, and trying people entirely outside regular governmental channels. Also in 1393, at the very time when the Lan Yü case was at its peak of intensity, T'ai-tsu proclaimed that prosecutions of persons implicated in the old Hu Wei-yung affair of 1380 should now terminate; all alleged accomplices who had not yet been punished were pardoned. Then in 1395 T'ai-tsu issued a proclamation rationalizing his past use of notoriously irregular and vicious punishments and banning them for the future:

> Since the time when we first commenced to undertake military action more than forty years have passed. We have personally ordered all the affairs of the realm, and there are no cases of human goodness and evil, honesty and falseness, to which we have not turned our attention. Among these we have indeed encountered many persons whose flagrant treachery and evil were beyond doubting, and we have specially ordered extra-legal punishments for them. Our intent has been to teach people about that from which they should be deterred by fear of the consequences, so that they would not readily violate the laws. However, this special power has been only temporarily instituted, in order to deal with the incorrigibly treacherous; it is not a method which a ruler who maintains the precedents [of the past] would adopt permanently. Hereafter successive emperors in ruling the realm will adhere exclusively to the regulations of the Great Code [i.e., the Ming Code], and will not be permitted to employ . . . [various corporal punishments] . . . Should any official ever propose the employment of such punishments, all civil and military officials shall immediately impeach him, and he shall be severely punished.[29]

But T'ai-tsu never mellowed completely. The very next year he angrily ordered the censor Wang P'u 王朴 killed for having repeatedly disagreed with him. When Wang had already been taken to the execution ground, T'ai-tsu summoned him back and demanded whether he had changed his mind. Wang, always blunt, replied, "After Your Majesty esteemed me sufficiently to appoint me a censor, how could I have failed him to such an extent! If I were guiltless, I could hardly have been sentenced to death. If I am guilty, how then could I be allowed to live? Today I want no more than to die promptly." T'ai-tsu, newly enraged, ordered

the execution carried out cruelly; but he shouted to the attending imperial diarists, wrily and perhaps with some rue, "Let it be recorded
that on this date the emperor murdered the guiltless censor [Wang] P'u!"

With very few exceptions, all the men who had helped T'ai-tsu
attain the throne and establish his dynasty--and who, as the Chinese
have traditionally reckoned, were not fortunate enough to die in battle
or to die of natural causes early--were got out of T'ai-tsu's way in
these purges, and their families were ruined. Li Shan-ch'ang, the
legalistically inclined civilian adviser who was perhaps most responsible
for T'ai-tsu's socioeconomic rehabilitation policies, was allowed the
privilege of committing suicide in 1390 rather than be tried for alleged
complicity in the Hu Wei-yung case. The marshal Fu Yu-te was similarly allowed to commit suicide in 1394 when, fearing implication in the
Lan Yü case, he made some rash statements that gave T'ai-tsu offense.
One of the emperor's own sons, the prince of T'an, killed his wife and
committed suicide in 1390 when he was summoned to an imperial inquiry
after some of his relatives by marriage had been put to death as accomplices of Hu Wei-yung. T'ai-tsu's boyhood friends and subsequent great
marshals Hsü Ta and T'ang Ho were the only major early supporters
who died in honored retirement, Hsü in 1385 and T'ang in 1395; and it
has always been rumored that T'ai-tsu secretly had even Hsü Ta
dispatched.

*   *   *   *   *

Many modern non-communist historians such as Meng Sen and
Li Chieh, while not condoning T'ai-tsu's cruelty and his capriciously
harsh treatment of those who served him, have been inclined to treat
him with overall lenience. Indeed, it is possible to understand T'ai-tsu
as a naturally rough man who, to his awed surprise, found it possible
to fight his way to power after a period of chaotic disorder, callous and
arrogant national leadership, and generally slipshod and oppressive
administration; who, on finding himself emperor of a newly united China,
became frantically jealous of his power, suspicious of those to whom
he must delegate it, and insecure in confrontation with the moral and
intellectual self-confidence of the literati class whose subtleties he
could not wholly comprehend; and who therefore resorted to terroristic
methods to ensure that his personal position remained unchallengeable
and that good government as he conceived it was not subverted. One
can admire T'ai-tsu's respect for the integrity of Yüan loyalists such
as the halfbreed general Kökö Temür or the Chinese civil official
Ts'ai Tzu-ying 蔡子英 , who upon being captured in 1376 refused to
acknowledge Ming rule or accept office in the Ming government even

under torture and who was finally escorted back to the Mongols in honor. One can also sympathize with T'ai-tsu's exasperation about the self-serving arrogance of some of his generals, about the corruption of some of his nouveau riche officials, and about the haughty ineptitude of such literati as the local educators Wu Ts'ung-ch'üan 吳從權 and Chang Heng 張恆, who while visiting Nanking in 1392 were questioned in audience about the sufferings of the people and responded, "Our duty is to teach scholars, and we are not acquainted with civil administration." T'ai-tsu angrily said, "Since you two do not understand worldly conditions among the people, what do you regularly teach? Even if you had promising students, they would be ruined by you!" He had both banished to remote posts. One can even accept that, given his personal background and the conditions of his time, the best T'ai-tsu could have done was to restore order and stability, as he did; and that a more gently benevolent man, failing in this inevitably, could have achieved nothing. Still, one can only regret that T'ai-tsu's achievements must be counterbalanced in the historical reckoning by ruthlessness on a scale unprecedented in the history of Chinese government and characteristic, as F. Münzel has suggested, of such modern totalitarian dictators as Hitler and Stalin, and by the imprint that he thereby left on Chinese government after his time.

IV. T'ai-tsu's Legacy: The Mature Ming Autocracy

When T'ai-tsu died in 1398 the Ming throne passed to a young grandson known to history as the Chien-wen 建文 emperor. A gentle and scholarly man, he set out to moderate T'ai-tsu's excesses and irregularities and to assert his own authority over his powerful uncles, T'ai-tsu's remaining sons. He was soon overthrown by his oldest surviving uncle, the prince of Yen, who in another long reign as the emperor Ch'eng-tsu, from 1402 into 1424, reasserted T'ai-tsu's style of government while modifying some of its forms. The national capital was moved permanently into the north, to Peking. There was a relaxation of T'ai-tsu's extreme centralization of power, with the emergence of provincial governors, multi-province supreme commanders, and especially a top-echelon Grand Secretariat at the capital. Palace eunuchs also steadily took more important roles in administration. After one further generation, by the middle of the fifteenth century, the full-dimensioned Ming autocracy had attained its mature characteristics.

Dynastic Disruption and Restoration

T'ai-tsu's consolidation of power in his own hands went beyond
the governmental reorganizations and the purges of powerful generals
and officials that have been described above. It included utilizing his
own sons, as soon as they were mature enough, to oversee military
matters throughout the empire, and especially along the northern frontier. The eldest son, Chu Piao 朱標, was named heir apparent at
the beginning of the Hung-wu era and, in accordance with the Chinese
tradition, was retained in Nanking for training so that he might succeed
his father with minimal disruption. Other sons were invested as imperial princes in groups, beginning in 1370; and as they matured they
"went to their fiefs" (chih-kuo 之 國)--that is, took up residence in
strategic cities where they had palaces, generous stipends, eunuch
attendants, and personal bodyguard units. Between 1378 and 1380
the second, third, and fourth sons thus established themselves at Sian
in Shensi (the prince of Ch'in), at T'ai-yüan in Shansi (the prince of
Chin), and at modern Peking, then called Peiping (the prince of Yen).
Others of T'ai-tsu's twenty-six sons (all except one who died in infancy)
scattered to their assigned fiefs in the following years. They were not
expected to take any part in routine governmental administration. However, during the 1380s they served apprenticeships in military command
under the frontier generals. Then, in 1390 the princes of Chin and Yen
were sent out in command of a patrolling expedition beyond the Great
Wall, and in 1393 they were ordered to take supervisory control over
the defense forces of the central section of the northern frontier. In
this way military control over the empire was being transferred from
the great marshals of the early Hung-wu era, now disappearing from
public life, to imperial princes. Through the 1390s the prince of Yen
in particular regularly campaigned in Inner Mongolia. Similarly,
princes elsewhere were assigned to command forces that quelled an
uprising among the Man aborigines of Hukuang province in 1397.

The death of the heir apparent in 1392 precipitated an awkward
and delicate decision. His brothers, especially the frontier princes,
were powerfully armed, well rooted in strategic bases, and jealous if
not ambitious. This was especially true of the prince of Yen, who had
approximately one hundred thousand experienced troops under his direct
command, was known to be manufacturing firearms and other heavy
military gear at Peking, and was even issuing his own paper money.
T'ai-tsu was both annoyed at and proud of him; the prince of Yen was
unquestionably the old emperor's favorite son. Although official
records give no evidence to this effect, T'ai-tsu could hardly have

avoided giving serious consideration to naming the prince of Yen his new heir apparent in 1392. To do so, however, T'ai-tsu would have had to pass over and probably alienate the older princes of Ch'in and Chin; and, even were this complication to be disregarded, strong traditions required succession in a direct line from eldest son to eldest son. In the end, T'ai-tsu complied with tradition and named Chu Piao's eldest son, Chu Yün-wen 朱允炆, his new heir apparent. Subsequently he discussed problems of succession in such circumstances with this grandson, then only fifteen years old, and apparently assured him of protective arrangements that would prevent future trouble, but none were ever made.

When T'ai-tsu's death brought Chu Yün-wen to the throne in 1398 at the age of twenty-one, many of his princely uncles, predictably, found the situation unpalatable. The princes of Ch'in and Chin had died in 1395 and 1398, respectively. The prince of Yen was now the senior member of the imperial clan, and he had no difficulty in rallying other uneasy princes to share his resentment.

The young new emperor Chu Yün-wen, known by his posthumous title Hui-ti 惠帝 as well as by the term "the Chien-wen emperor" deriving from his era-name, being forewarned, had already consulted about the problem of the princes with his tutorial advisers and had decided upon a general policy of "getting rid of the frontier feudatories" (hsiao-fan 削藩). Especially under the influence of a Hanlin Academy literatus, Huang Tzu-ch'eng 黃子澄, and an official of the Ministry of War, Ch'i T'ai 齊泰, he concluded not to take initial action directly against the prince of Yen but first to dispose of the less powerful malcontents and thus isolate Yen. Within two months after T'ai-tsu's death, in late summer of 1398, the prince of Chou, based at Kaifeng, was arrested for treason and exiled to live as a commoner in Yunnan. In 1399, in succession, the princes of Tai (in Shensi), Ch'i (in Shantung), and Min (in Szechwan) were all imprisoned or exiled, and the prince of Hsiang (in Hukuang) committed suicide rather than answer an imperial summons. In late summer of 1399 the prince of Yen decided to wait no longer and rebelled, announcing it was his duty and intention to rescue the inexperienced and impressionable young emperor from the influence of such evil counselors as Huang Tzu-ch'eng and Ch'i T'ai. From then until 1402 civil war ravaged western Shantung and the northern Huai basin, as the rebellious forces and the imperial armies fought inconclusively. The war ended only when the prince of Yen broke through imperial defenses in the north early in 1402, dashed down the Grand Canal zone almost unopposed, crossed the Yangtze, and was welcomed into Nanking by defectors in midsummer.

Information about the Chien-wen reign is meager and unreliable, since it was carefully edited by historiographers in the service of the new emperor Ch'eng-tsu. Official Ming accounts do not even acknowledge that there was such a reign; they extend the Hung-wu era through 1402, as if the Chien-wen emperor had been an illegitimate usurper. It was not until late in the sixteenth century that pardons were finally conferred posthumously on all loyal supporters of Chu Yün-wen, whom Ch'eng-tsu had slaughtered with all their relatives. These conditions no doubt screen from us many of the governmental policies that the unfortunate Chien-wen emperor advocated, but certain aspects of his reign are clear. He esteemed the literati class and wanted to rectify T'ai-tsu's oppressive ruler-minister imbalances. Counseled by a famous litterateur of the Hanlin Academy, Fang Hsiao-ju 方孝孺, he restructured the central government symbolically by reviving antique titles out of the ancient classic <u>Chou Li</u> for its agencies and offices, and probably intended to undertake a more substantive restructuring when opportunity afforded. The young emperor apparently also tried to alleviate some of the socioeconomic inequities inherited from T'ai-tsu. He ordered large numbers of men released from hereditary military service, freed many convicts, remitted half of all land taxes for 1399, and ordered equalization of the high taxes T'ai-tsu had imposed on the Yangtze delta region. It also seems clear that the Chien-wen emperor strictly enforced T'ai-tsu's regulations concerning palace eunuchs, whom T'ai-tsu himself had given ever greater responsibilities despite his own prohibitions; eunuchs were among the first and most useful defectors to the prince of Yen.

It is sometimes suggested that T'ai-tsu had so reduced the available pool of competent officials and officers by his purges that there was no one on whom his young successor could rely for protection against his uncles. The three-year civil war does indeed seem to have been undistinguished by brilliant generalship or heroic dedication; but this can be said of both sides. The Nanking government obviously underestimated the threat posed by the prince of Yen and was not adequately prepared for the war. On the other hand, the prince of Yen seems to have been under the almost hypnotic influence of a strange Buddhist monk named Tao-yen 道衍 who had devoted his life to the study of military strategy; and the Peking forces were apparently very slow to realize the unpreparedness and weakness of the imperial armies. Until it became clear in 1402 that the Peking forces would prevail, neither side seems to have attracted enthusiastic popular support.

When Nanking was about to fall, the imperial palace caught fire and burned down. Remains of the Chien-wen emperor were eventually

located in the ruins and buried. Soon, however, it was rumored that
the young emperor had in fact escaped from the capital in disguise as
a monk, and from time to time thereafter there were new rumors about
his wanderings. The new emperor Ch'eng-tsu took these rumors
seriously enough so that throughout his twenty-two year reign he had
agents scouring the empire for any possible trace of his nephew. Legends
(and some historians) recount that long afterwards, in 1440, an aged
man identified as Chu Yün-wen was brought to the capital and died the
same year in the seclusion of the palace. Throughout the remainder of
the Ming dynasty the Chinese people apparently liked to hear romantic
yarns about the Chien-wen emperor's escape and subsequent adventures;
plays and novels on this theme were popular in late Ming years. But
the truth of the matter seems to be that no one can be sure what happened
to the doomed young emperor in 1402. Since there is no credible evidence that he ever publicly reappeared, the likelihood is that he did
not survive the fall of Nanking.

*   *   *   *   *

Ch'eng-tsu became third Ming emperor at the age of forty-two.
His personal name was Chu Ti 朱棣. His reign-era, covering the
years 1403 through 1424, was auspiciously called Yung-lo 永樂 ("Eter-
nal Joy"). Immediately after his death he was given the temple name
T'ai-tsung 太宗 ("Grand Ancestor"), which had traditionally been used
for strong second emperors in Chinese dynasties; but in 1538 his temple
name was changed to Ch'eng-tsu 成祖 ("Completing Ancestor"), which
appropriately suggests that he brought to fulfillment what his father
T'ai-tsu had begun. He was probably the natural son of a Korean concubine in T'ai-tsu's palace. Be that as it may, he was a big, vigorous,
active man in his father's style, equally harsh when offended but less
inclined to irrational rages and more self-confident in handling his
subordinates. His reign was a busy and important one.

Ch'eng-tsu lost no time in revoking all the revisionist reforms
that the Chien-wen emperor had promulgated and in purging loyal
Chien-wen supporters, including Huang Tzu-ch'eng, Ch'i T'ai, and
Fang Hsiao-ju. Thousands perished. The one major Chien-wen policy
that Ch'eng-tsu perpetuated was to weaken the feudatory princes. Many
of the princedoms in the north were transferred into central or southern
China during the early Yung-lo years; in other instances, the military
bodyguard units of princes were dismantled or drastically reduced.
The princely establishments came to be firmly under the control of
administrators appointed by the emperor and answerable to him. From
this time on, imperial princes were seldom more than ornamental
symbols expensively maintained in the major cities of the empire with

only ceremonial functions. In these ways Ch'eng-tsu secured control over both the civil administration and the military establishment and delivered it into the hands of his own appointees. By the end of his reign China was stably consolidated, and the dynasty was never again to be disturbed significantly by challenges from within the government or the imperial clan. In attaining such stability Ch'eng-tsu had not resorted to sustained wholesale purges approaching the awesome dimensions of T'ai-tsu's great pogroms, and the empire had settled down rather rapidly into a less anxious, more productive normalcy under the general administrative and socioeconomic guidelines set forth by T'ai-tsu. Among the more notable achievements and developments of the Yung-lo era are the following:

1. Ch'eng-tsu's personal power base was in the north, and northern frontier problems had been uppermost in his mind throughout his early training as prince of Yen. Moreover, in part because of China's embroilment in domestic troubles during the Chien-wen reign, the Mongols were showing signs of recovering from the thorough batterings T'ai-tsu had given them. Ch'eng-tsu consequently was determined to move the national capital northward, and as early as 1403 he transformed the former Peiping province into a metropolitan area similar in its administrative organization to the area around Nanking; it was now officially named Northern Capital (Peking). While necessarily having to spend much time overseeing the central government at Nanking, Ch'eng-tsu visited his old base in the north as often as possible, and he particularly made it the main headquarters of the northern defense system. In 1407 he officially authorized eventual transfer of the central government to Peking, and from 1409 on he spent most of his time there, leaving his heir apparent in charge of a regency council at Nanking. In 1417 large-scale work began on palace reconstruction in Peking, and thereafter Ch'eng-tsu never again visited Nanking. The new palace was completed in 1420, and on New Year's Day of 1421 Peking formally became national capital, as it remained through the rest of the Ming dynasty and throughout the subsequent Ch'ing dynasty as well. The northern metropolitan area now became "the capital," and Nanking an auxiliary capital with a skeletal replica of the central government; its surrounding area now became known as the Southern Metropolitan Area (Nan chih-li).

2. Before moving the national capital to Peking Ch'eng-tsu had to make new arrangements for the transport of grain supplies from the Yangtze valley to the north. Agricultural rehabilitation on the North

China Plain and the development of military colonies and the so-
called merchants' colonies along the frontiers had developed so
satisfactorily that the hazardous sea transport of grain around the
Shantung peninsula was abandoned at the beginning of the Yung-lo
era. But the gradual transfer of palace and central government
personnel and functions to Peking, combined with military campaigns that Ch'eng-tsu mounted against the reorganizing Mongols,
enormously increased the need for grain in the north. As early as
1404 the naval commander Ch'en Hsüan 陳瑄, who had surrendered
the Yangtze defense fleet to Ch'eng-tsu in 1402, was ordered to
resume the sea transport and to deliver one million piculs of grain
annually to the Peking area. At the same time, inland waterways
were used as fully as possible, although the long-unused Grand
Canal was silted up at many points and troublesome porterages kept
inland transport expensive. Ch'en Hsüan's sea transport operations,
on the other hand, were spectacularly successful. Even so, in 1411
major reconstruction work was ordered on the Grand Canal, and by
the end of that first year sea transport vessels were provided safe
entry directly into the Yellow River mouth, so that they need no longer
go around Shantung. Then Ch'en Hsüan undertook to rehabilitate
the southern sections of the old Grand Canal, between the Yellow
River and the Yangtze. He accomplished some remarkable engineering feats, including construction of forty-seven locks. In 1415
this work was completed and the sea transport system was permanently abandoned. With Ch'en Hsüan serving as supreme commander
of the Grand Canal system until his death in 1433, the new military-
operated waterways system, extending from Hangchow northward to
T'ung-chou outside Peking, was able to deliver grain supplies in
quantities adequate for the northern needs. In 1421, when Peking
became national capital, deliveries began to exceed three million
piculs annually, and more than six million piculs were delivered
in 1432.[30]

3. In early Ming times the eastern parts of modern Manchuria were
occupied by proto-Manchus descended directly or indirectly from
the Chin dynasty Jurchen tribes. They had come under nominal
Ming control after the defeat and surrender of the Mongol warlord
in the northeast, Naghacu, in 1387; but when Ch'eng-tsu seized the
throne the Jurchen were more under the influence of Korea than of
China. Ch'eng-tsu undertook strenuous diplomatic initiatives to woo
the Jurchen and persuade them to accept effective Chinese overlordship. He offered them substantial trading opportunities and
organized them into nominal wei-so units of the Ming military

establishment. By 1410 Chinese influence had become paramount
in Manchuria, and Ming envoys had been acknowledged as far away
as Nurgan (Nu-erh-kan) near the mouth of the Amur River. Although
modern Chinese writers have made much of Yung-lo expansionism
into far Manchuria and parts of modern Siberia, there is little evidence of substantial direct Chinese activity in the region. The
Jurchen became peaceful trading partners under loose Chinese
suzerainty, and even this relationship deteriorated after Ch'eng-
tsu's time.[31]

4. By the end of the fourteenth century the Mongols north and west of
    China were roughly identifiable in three groups, the easternmost of
    which was called the Urianghad (Wu-liang-ha 兀 良 哈). These
    tribes, probably a mixture of Mongol and Jurchen elements, had
    surrendered to China after the military successes of Hsü Ta and
    Lan Yü in the 1380s and had been encouraged to settle peacefully in
    the region of modern Jehol province, between the Great Wall and
    the Liao River of Manchuria. They accepted Chinese-style organ-
    ization, under their own chiefs, in three military guard units called
    To-yen, T'ai-ning, and Fu-yü; and they were kept under the close
    supervision of a Peiping Branch Regional Military Commission and
    the prince of Ning, both headquartered among them at Ta-ning. At
    the outset of his rebellion against Nanking, Ch'eng-tsu had rushed
    troops into this region to secure his rear, and Urianghad cavalry
    had been valuable allies in his rebellion. In recognition of their
    services, Ch'eng-tsu in effect granted them independence by with-
    drawing the Peiping Branch Regional Military Commission within
    the Great Wall to Pao-ting (modern Hopei province) and similarly
    transferring the Ning princedom into the interior; and he annually
    sent the Urianghad chiefs substantial gifts. His conciliatory policy
    toward the Urianghad Mongols, as in the case of the Jurchen beyond
    them, was generally effective for his own reign; but his policy
    toward the Urianghad tribes had isolated the Liao-tung outpost and
    had exposed the Peking region to future Mongol threats from the
    area immediately beyond the Great Wall.

5. The other Mongol groups with which Ch'eng-tsu had significant con-
    tacts were the remnants of the old Yüan imperial forces, whom the
    Chinese now consistently called the Tatars (Ta-tan), often referred
    to by Western writers as the Eastern Mongols; and a newly emerging
    group of Western Mongols or Oirat (Wa-la 瓦 剌), who in subse-
    quent centuries came to be called such varied names as the Kalmuks,
    the Eleuths, and the Dzungars. Even beyond these, far in the west

at Samarkand, was Tamerlane, who had already invaded and pillaged both India and Syria when Ch'eng-tsu came to the Chinese throne. In 1404, Tamerlane prepared to launch an expedition eastwards against China. Vaguely aware of this, Ch'eng-tsu alerted his western commanders in Kansu to be prepared for trouble, but Tamerlane died in 1405 and the expedition was canceled. Thereafter Ch'eng-tsu maintained amicable diplomatic relations with Tamerlane's heirs at Samarkand and Herat, keeping the Central Asian trade routes open. As for the Tatars and the Oirat Mongols, neither were powerful enough to do more than struggle among themselves during the early Yung-lo years when Ch'eng-tsu was busy consolidating his rule in China proper; and Ch'eng-tsu maintained his defenses while exchanging polite messages with the Mongol chiefs. Beginning in 1410, however, he resumed the aggressive extramural patrolling to which he had earlier, as a prince, been accustomed. In 1410, 1414, 1422, 1423, and 1424 the emperor personally led grand armies northward into the Gobi, primarily against the Tatar chief Arughtai (A-lu-t'ai 阿魯台), but occasionally against the Oirat and even against troublesome Urianghad groups. The campaigns resulted in some battles in which Ming forces won indecisive victories, but their chief effect was to keep the different Mongol groups on the defensive and to prevent the emergence of a reunited Mongol empire under a new grand khan on China's frontier. Astute diplomacy on Ch'eng-tsu's part also helped keep the Mongols divided during this period. It was while returning from the last of his campaigns northward that Ch'eng-tsu fell ill and died in 1424, beyond the Great Wall.

6. China's southern neighbor Annam (modern North Vietnam) had been in domestic trouble since the 1370s. In 1400 the young heir to its Tran dynasty was deposed by his regent grandfather Le Qui-ly 黎 季犛 , and a new Ho dynasty was proclaimed. Ch'eng-tsu, from the beginning of his reign, was called upon by Annamese refugees to restore legitimate rule in their country. Le Qui-ly prepared to resist, harassed China's southern borders, and finally in 1406 murdered Chinese diplomatic envoys. Ch'eng-tsu then decided to intervene. A large invasion force was organized in Kwangsi and Yunnan and pressed straight southward by land routes, overwhelming Annamite defenses and capturing the Ho dynasty capital. Since no Tran heir seemed readily available for enthronement, and since some Annamites petitioned to be incorporated directly into the Ming empire, Ch'eng-tsu in 1407 made Annam into a new Chinese province, called Chiao-chih 交阯. Among the fruits of the conquest of

Annam were some nine thousand educated Annamese who were
imported for government appointments in China, including men who
introduced new, more effective firearms into the Chinese arsenal.
But the conquest had few other advantages for China. No sooner
had the invasion army withdrawn than patriotic Annamese began
rebelling against their new governors. Control was maintained
only by extraordinary service on the part of two Chinese: Chang
Fu 張輔 the general who had led the original invasion and who
was repeatedly reassigned there between 1407 and 1416; and Huang
Fu 黃福, a civil official who accompanied the invasion expedition
and from 1407 until after Ch'eng-tsu's death in 1424 remained as
combined administration and surveillance commissioner-in-chief
of the new province. Beginning in 1418 guerrilla resistance led by
Le Loi 黎利 undermined the provincial administration to such an
extent that at Ch'eng-tsu's death the Chinese position in Annam was
most precarious--in fact, as events quickly proved, doomed.

7. More than any other ruler in history, Ch'eng-tsu promoted the overseas extension of Chinese authority. In 1403, by virtue of changing
circumstances in Japan rather than his own doings, he became the
first Chinese emperor ever acknowledged as suzerain by the
Japanese. Prolonged political disunity in Japan, among other
things, had foiled T'ai-tsu's early efforts to make the Japanese
curb their piratical raids on the Chinese coast. Continuing raids,
and finally the alleged effort by chief councilor Hu Wei-yung to find
support in Japan for a Chinese rebellion, had provoked T'ai-tsu to
terminate official relations between the two countries in 1382. But
in 1392 Japan was reunified, albeit loosely, under the Ashikaga
shogunate; and by the time of Ch'eng-tsu's enthronement the new
Japanese central government was eager to put Sino-Japanese relations on a regular, profitable basis. A Japanese embassy therefore arrived in China in 1403 with a message from the shogun
referring to himself as a "subject" of China and suggesting restoration of amicable relations. Ch'eng-tsu was willing to be conciliatory,
and in 1404 what amounted to a commercial agreement was worked
out, allowing Japanese fleets to appear at Ningpo once every three
years with tribute and trade goods. In 1405, 1408, and 1410 the
shogunate even sent captured Japanese pirates to the Chinese court
for punishment. The succession of a new shogun in 1408, however,
brought a gradual change of attitude in Japan; and from 1411 on, no
tribute missions came from Japan despite Ch'eng-tsu's polite in-
quiries, and coastal raiding resumed. Like T'ai-tsu before him,
Ch'eng-tsu then threatened to send expeditionary forces to punish

the Japanese if they would not reform. But in 1419, when the shogunate harshly denied responsibility for the coastal raiders and
brusquely refused to resume the former tributary relationship,
Ch'eng-tsu did nothing further about the matter.[32]

8. Ch'eng-tsu is probably best known in world history for his sponsor-
ship of other overseas activities, in the southern oceans. The
reasons why he initiated unprecedented naval activities in this direction are not at all clear. It is possible that he originally intended
merely, if rather grandiosely, to send traditional announcements
of the accession of a new emperor as far afield as possible, or
that he wanted to stimulate the flow of overseas trading wealth into
China. Traditionally, historians have interpreted his overseas
expeditions as efforts to trace the Chien-wen emperor, since some
rumors indicated he had escaped abroad. Once initiated, the expeditions proved gratifying and profitable enough to be continued; if
nothing else, the ferrying back and forth of tribute bearers from
far overseas made the expeditions almost self-perpetuating. The
expeditions began in 1403, when at least three fleets were dispatched
from the Yangtze to Java, Calicut in south India, and intermediate
stops, apparently all under the command of eunuchs. In 1415 and
probably again in 1420 the eunuch Hou Hsien 侯顯, who between
1403 and 1427 also made several overland journeys to Tibet and
Nepal, took fleets to India. Most famous of all Ch'eng-tsu's ocean
admirals was the Moslem eunuch Cheng Ho 鄭和, who had entered
Ch'eng-tsu's personal service at Peking in the 1380s as a boy.
Ch'eng-tsu put him in charge of a grand armada of more than three
hundred capital ships, some reportedly measuring 440 feet in
length and 186 feet abeam, carrying 27,800 men as well as a rich
cargo, which left the Yangtze in midsummer of 1405 and returned
in 1407, having visited various states of Southeast Asia and south
India and having pacified the strategic Malacca straits by capturing
a piratical chief of Palembang on Sumatra. Other great voyages
followed in 1407-1409, 1409-1411, 1413-1415, 1417-1419, and 1421-
1422; and a final one after Ch'eng-tsu's time was undertaken in
1431-1433. During these voyages Cheng Ho visited no fewer than
thirty-seven countries, including some as far away as the Persian
Gulf, the Red Sea, and the east coast of Africa almost as far south
as Zanzibar. One of his lieutenants on the final voyage reached
Mecca. On the voyage of 1407-1409 Cheng Ho intervened in a civil
war in Java and established a new king; on the voyage of 1409-1411
he captured the hostile king of Ceylon and took him prisoner to
China; and on the voyage of 1413-1415 he helped a regional king on

Sumatra put down a rebellion. For all the states he visited Cheng
Ho brought home envoys bearing tribute to acknowledge Ch'eng-tsu's
overlordship. The tribute included strange animals such as giraffes,
lions, leopards, ostriches, zebras, and rhinoceroses, which fas-
cinated the Ming court and were sensational exhibits in the imperial
zoo.[33]

* * * * *

Thirteen more Ming emperors succeeded Ch'eng-tsu on the throne
at Peking as follows:

Jen-tsung 仁宗 : Chu Kao-chih 朱高熾, son of Ch'eng-tsu;
born in 1378, reigned 1424-1425; era-name Hung-hsi 洪熙

Hsüan-tsung 宣宗 : Chu Chan-chi 朱瞻基, son of Jen-tsung;
b. 1398, r. 1425-1435; era-name Hsüan-te 宣德

Ying-tsung 英宗 : Chu Ch'i-chen 朱祁鎮, son of Hsüan-tsung;
b. 1427, r. 1435-1449, era-name Cheng-t'ung 正統 ; restored 1457-
1464, era-name T'ien-shun 天順

Ching-ti 景帝 : Chu Ch'i-yü 朱祁鈺, brother of Ying-tsung;
b. 1428, r. 1449-1457; era-name Ching-t'ai 景泰

Hsien-tsung 憲宗 : Chu Chien-shen 朱見深, son of Ying-tsung;
b. 1447, r. 1464-1487; era-name Ch'eng-hua 成化

Hsiao-tsung 孝宗 : Chu Yu-t'ang 朱祐樘, son of Hsien-tsung;
b. 1470, r. 1487-1505; era-name Hung-chih 弘治

Wu-tsung 武宗 : Chu Hou-chao 朱厚照, son of Hsiao-tsung;
b. 1491, r. 1505-1521; era-name Cheng-te 正德

Shih-tsung 世宗 : Chu Hou-tsung 朱厚熜, cousin of Wu-tsung;
b. 1507, r. 1521-1566; era-name Chia-ching 嘉靖

Mu-tsung 穆宗 : Chu Tsai-kou 朱載垕, son of Shih-tsung;
b. 1537, r. 1566-1572; era-name Lung-ch'ing 隆慶

Shen-tsung 神宗 : Chu I-chün 朱翊鈞, son of Mu-tsung;
b. 1563, r. 1572-1620; era-name Wan-li 萬曆

Kuang-tsung 光宗 : Chu Ch'ang-lo 朱常洛, son of Shen-tsung;
b. 1582, r. only one month in 1620; era-name T'ai-ch'ang 泰昌

Hsi-tsung 熹宗 : Chu Yu-chiao 朱由校, son of Kuang-tsung;
b. 1605, r. 1620-1627; era-name T'ien-ch'i 天啓

Chuang-lieh-ti 莊烈帝, also known as Ssu-tsung 思宗, Huai-
tsung 懷宗, and I-tsung 毅宗 : Chu Yu-chien 朱由檢, brother of
Hsi-tsung; b. 1611, r. 1627-1644; era-name Ch'ung-chen 崇禎

After Ch'eng-tsu's strenuous and costly activities in Mongolia
and overseas, the Chinese were ready to relax. Lo Jung-pang has even
suggested that they succumbed to a sort of national lethargy.[34] The
immediate successors, Jen-tsung and Hsüan-tsung, were particularly.
conscientious, humane, and unaggressive rulers. They concentrated
on domestic affairs and are traditionally considered to have provided
the most stable and effective administration of the whole dynasty.
Hsüan-tsung accepted the abandonment of Annam in 1428, acknowledging
the rebellious Le Loi as legitimate ruler there; restored amicable relations with Japan in 1432; terminated the ambitious overseas voyages of
Cheng Ho and others; and moved the northern outpost K'ai-p'ing back
from the old Mongol capital Shang-tu to a new location within the Great
Wall, thus completing the abandonment of the extramural frontier lands
to the Mongols that had begun with Ch'eng-tsu's granting a kind of independence to the Urianghad tribes. The legacy of T'ai-tsu, reinforced by
Ch'eng-tsu and moderated by Jen-tsung and Hsüan-tsung, kept China
generally peaceful, stable, and prosperous until early in the seventeenth
century, when cumulative governmental neglectfulness and socioeconomic
inequities so weakened the state that the Manchus, under strong leadership, were able to take control in the northeast and finally, in 1644,
supplant the Ming central government at Peking. In the interval, the
only major dynastic crisis had occurred in 1449, when the weak emperor
Ying-tsung was led on a vainglorious expedition into Mongolia by a dictatorial eunuch, Wang Chen 王振, and was defeated and captured at
T'u-mu 土木 by the Oirat chieftan Esen 也先. With Peking under
siege, the government was pulled together by a famous minister of war,
Yü Ch'ien 于謙, and stability was restored quickly under the interim
emperor Ching-ti.

By the time of the disastrous T'u-mu campaign of 1449, the Ming
governmental style had reached full maturity. T'ai-tsu's extreme
centralization of power in the emperor's hands had gradually been
modified, without significant change in the unbalanced ruler-minister
relationship; and palace eunuchs had become a major, if irregular,
element in government.

Limited Decentralization of Authority

T'ai-tsu's fragmentation of authority both in the central and provincial governments, so that no one man could function either as a prime minister or as a provincial governor, could not have been expected to survive as the empire settled into stable administrative routines. Coordination at various levels was imperative; and later, perhaps less diligent, and certainly less suspicious emperors gradually relinquished some of their inherited, excessively centralized powers. But it is noteworthy that, in this process, they did not formally change the structure of government bequeathed by T'ai-tsu. Instead, coordinating officials were established in the guise of ad hoc, makeshift expedients; and so they remained, never acquiring the institutionalized stability that might have made their positions potential bases for challenges to the imperial authority. Their powers fluctuated with the changing personalities of the individuals involved, officials and emperors alike.

At the provincial level, the need for coordination of the provincial administration office, the provincial surveillance office, the regional military commission, and often the tactically oriented regional commander gradually brought into being imperial delegates whose powers clearly fell short of those that would be suggested by the title provincial governor. In 1392, as has been noted, T'ai-tsu had sent his heir apparent to "tour and soothe" (hsün-fu) the northwest. This gesture served as a precedent for Ch'eng-tsu in 1421, during the administratively disruptive period following the removal of the national capital from Nanking to Peking, to send a total of twenty-six high-ranking capital officials to tour various parts of the empire, "pacifying and soothing" (an-fu) the troops and the populace. In subsequent years high-ranking ministerial and censorial officials were often sent out on such missions, in some cases "touring and inspecting" (hsün-shih), and in others, when there were military crises to be dealt with, serving as grand defenders (chen-shou).

Under Hsüan-tsung, in 1430, the sending of metropolitan dignitaries out on such temporary commissions fell into a regular pattern. "Touring pacifiers" (hsün-fu) began to appear as resident coordinators in the various provinces and, in addition, in special frontier zones and other strategic places, with indefinite tenure extending sometimes, during the remainder of the dynasty, to ten or even twenty years. The title of these dignitaries might best be rendered grand coordinator, though in practice it is often translated as provincial governor, even when the territorial jurisdiction did not coincide with a province. Such an official generally supervised the administration of the territory under his jurisdiction. In a province, he "controlled" (chieh-chih 節制) the regular top-level provincial authorities. Once each year, as a general rule, he was expected to travel to the capital to report and deliberate on current affairs.

The grand coordinator was concerned with both civil and military affairs, as local circumstances demanded. When military affairs were a significant element in his jurisdiction, he was normally designated grand coordinator and concurrent superintendent of military affairs. In an area where there was also a military-service regional commander, he was normally designated grand coordinator and concurrent associate in military affairs.

Grand coordinators came to be delegated to every province--to Chekiang, Honan, Shantung, Hukuang, Szechwan, Kiangsi, Shansi, and Shensi in the early 1430s; to Yunnan in 1444; to Kweichow (which Ch'eng-tsu had given provincial status in 1413) in 1449; to Kwangtung intermittently until 1566 (then abolished in 1570); to Kwangsi intermittently until 1569; and to Fukien in 1556. Others were assigned to other specially defined territories--in 1497 to the area of Nan-kan 南贛, the rugged terrain in which the three provinces Kwangtung, Kiangsi, and Hukuang converged, far from any of the three provincial capitals; and in 1597, during a struggle with the Japanese in Korea, to the area around Tientsin, the strategic coastal gateway to Peking. In addition, grand coordinators were assigned to the vital defense-command areas along the northern frontier--Kansu, Ning-hsia, Yen-sui, Hsüan-fu, and Liao-tung in 1435-1436, and two zones immediately northwest and north-east of Peking later in the fifteenth century. In the seventeenth century, when the Manchus began to press upon the Ming northern frontier, the number of grand coordinators increased bewilderingly.

The positions of grand coordinators were never recognized in Ming times as substantive appointments. They were always special deputations of men who had substantive (though in this case nonfunctional) appointments in regular metropolitan agencies, usually as vice ministers in the six ministries. After 1453 they were regularly given nominal concurrent appointments as vice censors-in-chief or assistant censors-in-chief "so as to facilitate their affairs." Thus endowed with both ministerial and censorial titles, they had overtowering prestige. But their formal titles were very cumbersome--for example, vice minister of war and concurrent vice censor-in-chief serving as grand coordinator and concurrent associate in military affairs of Ning-hsia. Despite such titular associations, the grand coordinator was not considered a member of any particular governmental agency, nor did he have a prescribed staff of subordinate officials. He was considered a provincial-level surrogate of the emperor and was accountable to the emperor.

Out of the grand coordinator system there eventually evolved a similarly ad hoc institution of supreme commanders (tsung-tu), sometimes called viceroys. The supreme commander was a coordinator on an even larger scale, delegated on a temporary basis to deal with a particular military problem affecting several grand coordinators and regional commanders. In 1430 one vice minister and in 1451 one vice censor-in-chief were designated supreme commanders to supervise the collection and transport of grain taxes from the Yangtze valley to Peking. This designation became a continuing commission, subsuming a concurrent grand coordinatorship in the Huai-an area of the Huai basin. At times supreme commanders were commissioned for other kinds of nonmilitary supervision--for example, to direct water-control construction work along the Yellow River. But the institution was essentially a military one, beginning in 1441 with the delegation of a minister of war as supreme commander of military affairs to cope with a rebellion in Yunnan. From the late fifteenth century on, supreme commanders were increasingly delegated. Though some became more or less permanent fixtures of the government like the grand coordinators, most were transitory. Their territorial jurisdictions were sometimes so extensive as to include five provinces. At one time, an official was thus delegated to be supreme commander of Kiangsi, Chekiang, Fukien, Hukuang, and the southern metropolitan area; another once controlled Shensi, Shansi, Honan, Hukuang, and Szechwan simultaneously. Frequently, a supreme commander was concurrently grand coordinator of one of the provinces or other territories under his supervisory jurisdiction.

As was the case with grand coordinators, supreme commanders had substantive appointments in regular administrative agencies. Usually, they were nominally ministers of war and concurrent censors-in-chief. The full designation of a supreme commander might be a very complex one--for example, minister of war and concurrent censor-in-chief serving as supreme commander of military affairs in Kwangtung and Kwangsi and concurrently controlling military rations, additionally in charge of salt regulations, and concurrently grand coordinator of Kwangtung. During the last two decades of the Ming dynasty supreme commanders proliferated remarkably.[35]

* * * * *

Coordination of the central government agencies evolved in the same ad hoc pattern out of the low-ranking grand secretaries that T'ai-tsu had first established in the Hanlin Academy in 1382 to assist with the education of the heir apparent and serve as general consultants to the throne. Ch'eng-tsu began early to utilize grand secretaries in processing his administrative paperwork, and by the 1420s the grand secretaries were beginning to play an important executive role in the government.

Grand secretaries, nominally members of the Hanlin Academy, were assigned for duty to six designated buildings within the vast imperial palace. All six posts were not always filled, but the number of functioning grand secretaries seldom fell below three. Until the middle of the sixteenth century Ming documents identified them individually by their palace posts--for example, as grand secretary of the Hall of Literary Culture. Only thereafter did documents formalize the collective term nei-ko 內閣 (literally, "the palace pavilions") that is normally rendered into English as the Grand Secretariat; but it had been used informally since the reign of Ch'eng-tsu. In early times the grand secretaries seem actually to have functioned for the most part as individual counselors, being consulted and given responsibilities separately by the emperor, or at best in the loosest possible collegial group. Even after the middle of the sixteenth century they had only vaguely defined collective responsibilities; they then functioned as aides, still somewhat independent, to one unofficially recognized senior grand secretary (popularly called shou-fu 首輔). But as a new top-level executive group in the government, they were commonly referred to collectively as "the administration" (cheng-fu 政府).

The rise of grand secretaries to recognized executive authority was facilitated in 1424, when Jen-tsung gave his grand secretaries substantive appointments as high-ranking officials of regular administrative agencies, relegating their Hanlin posts to the status of concurrent appointments. To make their prestige even more secure, he also appointed them to elegant honorific titles carrying the highest rank available and good supplementary stipends. Thenceforth throughout the Ming period the men who were actually functioning as grand secretaries had their low Hanlin rank effectively obscured in this way; they always took ritual precedence over other civil officials by virtue of their high honorific ranks and their substantive (though in reality nominal) appointments in the administrative hierarchy, ordinarily as ministers or vice ministers in the six ministries.

In the emergence of the Grand Secretariat, as Tilemann Grimm has pointed out,[36] one must also note the fortuitous combination of emperors and ministers that appeared in the 1420s. Ch'eng-tsu's two immediate successors, Jen-tsung and Hsüan-tsung, were the first Ming emperors who had been carefully trained to rule by Confucian scholar-officials, and both had unprecedented respect for their literati advisers. Moreover, Hsüan-tsung could not but feel some awe toward men who had tutored his father and had served as grand secretaries under his grand-father Ch'eng-tsu as well as his father. The strong personalities of three such men, under the sympathetic rule of these emperors, shaped the Grand Secretariat into a stable institution despite its persisting informal status. These were "the three Yangs," whom later historians have consistently listed foremost among the great statesmen-officials of Ming times: Yang Shih-ch'i 楊士奇 (1365-1444), Yang Jung 楊榮 (1371-1440), and Yang P'u 楊溥 (1372-1446)--unrelated despite having identical surnames. Yang Shih-ch'i, generally renowned for his learning and character, and Yang Jung, for his political acumen, both joined Ch'eng-tsu's embryonic Grand Secretariat in 1402 and served continuously until their deaths in 1444 and 1440, respectively. Yang P'u, acclaimed for his integrity and constancy, tutored Jen-tsung early in the Yung-lo era and served as a grand secretary continuously from 1424 until his death in 1446. The relationship of these three grand secretaries with Jen-tsung, Hsüan-tsung, and especially with Jen-tsung's widow, the empress dowager Chang 張, who dominated the boy emperor Ying-tsung until her death in 1442, was unquestionably the most balanced and mutually respectful ruler-minister relationship of Ming history and perhaps of all Chinese history. Under the influence of the three Yangs, it became customary for important imperial decisions to be made only after deliberations and recommendations by assembled court officials (hui-i 會議). It also became customary for the grand secretaries (later, the senior grand secretary) to suggest appropriate responses to memorialized proposals by pasting to the face of each memorial a draft rescript for imperial approval (t'iao-chih 條旨, or p'iao-i 票擬). This technique of shaping imperial rescripts made possible, under inattentive later emperors, the exercise of almost dictatorial power over the government by such senior grand secretaries as the notoriously corrupt Yen Sung 嚴嵩 (1480-1565; in the Grand Secretariat 1542-1562) and the legalist-minded reformer Chang Chü-cheng 張居正 (1525-1582; in the Grand Secretariat 1567-1582).

The association of the grand secretaries with the Hanlin Academy embarrassed them in their relations with the rest of the officialdom and prevented their becoming regularized and effective successors of the former chief councilors or prime ministers. There was always a tension in Chinese imperial governments between what was called the "inner court" (nei-t'ing 內廷) and the "outer court" (wai-t'ing 外廷)-- that is, between the emperor and his intimately related service agencies on one hand and, on the other, the officialdom that administered the empire under imperial direction. The men who served in Ming times as functioning ministers or vice ministers in the six ministries were almost always men of long administrative experience, not only in the capital, but in the provinces as well. But the men selected to be grand secretaries almost invariably rose through a succession of Hanlin posts, broken only, if at all, by an appointment in some service or ceremonial agency such as the Ministry of Rites. To officials of the line administrative hierarchy, this meant that the grand secretaries had no roots in the outer court which they themselves embodied, but were representatives and spokesmen of the inner court. That is, the Grand Secretariat was considered a symbol and instrument of imperial authority, not of ministerial or bureaucratic authority. Grand secretaries, in consequence, often found themselves in the uneasy roles of mediators trusted neither by the emperors whom they served nor by the officialdom which they aspired to lead. What authority they attained, in either direction, was not inherent in their institutional roles but derived solely from the force of their personalities.[37]

*   *   *   *   *

With these modifications under Ch'eng-tsu and later emperors, the mature Ming government came to have the basic structure indicated in figure 3, in which the fine distinctions between different kinds of jurisdiction unfortunately cannot be illustrated.

Fig. 3. STRUCTURE OF THE MATURE MING GOVERNMENT

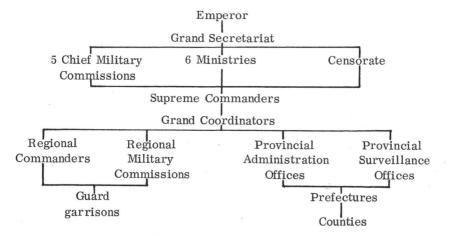

The bulk of routine governmental business was transacted, under guidelines established early in the dynasty, in reports and instructions that passed up and down the hierarchy between local and provincial authorities and the central government agencies. Grand coordinators and supreme commanders saw to it that national policies were implemented at the provincial level, under the watchful eyes of and to some extent in collaboration with regional inspectors sent out on one-year tours by the Censorate. Important business requiring imperial decisions, which might be initiated at any level in the hierarchy, was often referred to court deliberations and almost always filtered back to the administrative agencies in edicts or rescripts drafted by the Grand Secretariat. The mechanism seems to have worked smoothly and well, on the whole. Naturally, it had to be tinkered with and adjusted from time to time. Some senior grand secretaries wielded more influence than was considered proper by the outer court. There were predictable squabbles among groups of officials about policies and personalities, and at times these escalated into disruptive partisan feuds. But there were checks within the system--especially, surveillance and impeachment powers of the censorial agencies--that made it largely self-regulatory and were capable of keeping it in effective working order and responsive to the changing needs of the nation. On balance, historians have generally considered the Ming governmental system rather a marvel of institutional engineering. There were, however, disruptive intrusions that it could not cope with, on the part of abusive palace eunuchs and of wayward emperors themselves.

Eunuch Power and Its Abuses

The Ming dynasty was without doubt the high point in the history of eunuch influence in traditional Chinese government, and eunuch disruptiveness in Ming times has been the focus of much modern scholarly attention. The Chinese writer Ting I, especially, has portrayed Ming government in a highly sensational manner as a system that was dominated by institutionalized terrorism manipulated largely by eunuchs.[38] Exaggerated as his analysis may be, there can be no denying that Ming eunuchs repeatedly gained influence over emperors to such a degree that normal governmental procedures were seriously undermined.

Eunuchs were unambiguously members of the inner court, the only male attendants permitted to live in the imperial palace. They looked after the palace women and cooperated with them in satisfying the intimate, personal, everyday wants and needs of the emperor. They normally came from unprosperous classes in society and became eunuchs only to win wealth and power that were otherwise unattainable. Their status and rewards derived solely from faithful and pleasing service to their imperial master. Although these circumstances did not necessarily or normally make them depraved monsters, they were no doubt less affected by moralistic concerns or public opinion than were the officials who dominated the emperor's public life. Since it was only natural for emperors to seek relief from their heavy and constricting responsibilities and from the preachments of Confucian officials who were probably dour and seldom entertaining, eunuchs who were committed to cater to emperors' whims had unequaled opportunities to become their confidants. Despite the well-understood dangers of eunuch influence in government and repeated fulminations against it, it was inevitable that young or weak emperors would sometimes fall under the influence of strong-willed eunuchs and that dilatory emperors would sometimes use vigorous and clever eunuchs to do much of their work for them--for good or ill, as the case may be. When sullen and irresponsible emperors such as Shih-tsung in the sixteenth century and Shen-tsung at the beginning of the seventeenth century secluded themselves from the officialdom for years on end, eunuchs became go-betweens essential to the maintenance of basic governmental routine. At such times, imperial decisions were transmitted to the Grand Secretariat on papers carried by eunuchs shuttling in and out of the remote recesses of the palace, and sometimes they were even transmitted orally. Eunuch influence on state affairs was then almost unavoidable.

Despite T'ai-tsu's intention that the eunuch staff should not exceed one hundred persons, it did not remain at this low level. By the end of the fifteenth century eunuchs apparently numbered ten thousand; late in the sixteenth century they were regularly recruited in groups of more than three thousand at a time; and by the end of the dynasty it has been estimated their number had grown to more than seventy thousand. Even if this last figure is grossly inflated, as seems probable, palace eunuchs constituted a substantial group.

How eunuchs were recruited in Ming times is not wholly clear. Although self-castration was prohibited by Ming law, it was widely practiced throughout most of the dynasty by men seeking palace employment. Perhaps more commonly, influence-seeking parents of the lower classes with the good fortune of having several sons sometimes offered one young boy for palace service. This was permitted by law; but whether such boys suffered castration before or after their acceptance for service is not clear. At all events, since castration was not a statutory punishment in Ming times, the eunuch staff seems to have been recruited and regularly replenished through voluntary action on the part of the candidates or their parents.

As the number of eunuchs proliferated, so did the complex of agencies in which they were organized. The basic establishment consisted of twenty-four offices charged with various aspects of palace maintenance: the care of utensils, ceremonial equipment, apparel, stables, and seals; the provision of fuel, foodstuffs, music, paper, and baths; the handling of documents; the upkeep of buildings and grounds; and the manufacture of textiles, art objects, and other craft goods. Eunuchs also supervised the palace treasury. The most prestigious of all the eunuch agencies was the Directorate of Ceremonial (ssu-li chien), the director of which was the unchallenged chief of the palace staff.

For eunuchs to staff the palace establishment, even in large numbers, was normal in any Chinese dynasty. What was irregular in Ming times was use of eunuchs on assignments outside the palace and the capital. This practice upset the governmental system, since palace eunuchs were in the emperor's personal service and were not trained or acknowledged as agents of government in a broader sense. The line between acceptable and unacceptable utilization of eunuchs outside the palace must have been very difficult to draw, had the issue ever been faced squarely. For eunuchs to be sent on diplomatic missions, as they often were, was in itself not an obviously dangerous irregularity. Even for Cheng Ho to undertake his great ocean voyages, or for other eunuchs to be assigned to special military commands, might have been considered acceptable extensions of eunuchs' personal service to the emperor--as it were, extensions of the emperor's personal presence. This kind of thing began with T'ai-tsu himself. Ch'eng-tsu, as in the case of the Cheng Ho voyages, used eunuchs outside the palace on a much larger scale; and Hsüan-tsung, notwithstanding his excellent rapport with the officialdom, posted eunuch grand defenders--that is, supervisors of military affairs--throughout the empire.

In the eyes of the literati, there was far too much of such reliance on eunuchs, even if one might concede the point that it was personal service to the emperor rather than "eunuch interference in governmental affairs," which was prohibited by law and offensive to the prevailing ideology. Moreover, eunuchs under Ch'eng-tsu and later emperors came to have assignments as special tax collectors, directors of state-operated manufactories, supervisors of foreign trade, managers of imperially owned estates, and special investigators of every sort--assignments that intruded eunuchs directly into the regular governmental relationships among officials and between the officialdom and the people. Such use of eunuchs was greatly resented by the officialdom. U. H. Mammitzsch has written that "Ming emperors seem to have appreciated the informality and directness of eunuch employment over that of involving the regular bureaucracy. They provided the ruler with a convenient device to bypass the civilian bureaucracy and avoid the endless obstructions and moral exhortations that were the inevitable byproduct of the relationship between the emperor and his literati officials."[39] Just so; it was precisely this irregularity that officials resented, partly for obviously selfish reasons but partly on solid principle. It could be argued that eunuchs on such assignments, because of their special status as personal agents of the emperor, were not subject to the normal checks and restraints of the governmental establishment and therefore found it irresistibly tempting to abuse officials and the people as they liked.

The most resented eunuch activities were those of the agencies called the Eastern Depot (tung-ch'ang 東廠) and the Western Depot (hsi-ch'ang 西廠). These were openly acknowledged secret service organs charged with ferreting out unspecified treasonable activities on the part of anyone in the empire, wholly unrestrained by the regular governmental establishment. The Eastern Depot was established by Ch'eng-tsu in 1420 and remained the principal secret service organ thereafter. The Western Depot, similar and supplementary, was established in 1477. These eunuch agencies always collaborated with the emperor's personal bodyguard, the Embroidered-uniform Guard; their agents arrested, tortured, and tried victims without any resort to the regularly established judicial organs. Their influence waxed and waned in response to the personalities of the successive emperors, but they were a constant threat to the normal functioning of the state.

Within the palace, eunuchs also gained irregular powers after the early Ming decades by controlling the flow of documents to and from the emperor. T'ai-tsu's insistence that eunuchs be kept illiterate was ignored by Ch'eng-tsu, who assigned tutors to some eunuchs on an informal basis. Hsüan-tsung formalized the education of eunuchs by establishing a special school for them in the palace (nei-shu t'ang 內書堂); then in 1432 he appointed ten educated eunuchs to a new confidential secretariat (wen-shu fang 文書房), charged with handling his personal paperwork. Thus, at the very time when the Grand Secretariat was being shaped as a buffer between the central government and the emperor, yet another buffer was appearing between the Grand Secretariat and the emperor. The consequences have been summarized by Robert Crawford as follows:

In theory, the eunuchs were to approve the recommendations of the Grand Secretariat without change. If there was
something to be changed, it was to be returned to the Grand
Secretariat. In practice, however, after the period of
Hsüan-tsung, eunuchs were in a position to make their own
changes. In the transmission of instructions, they could
interpolate their own ideas or desires. Since the recommendations of the Grand Secretariat had to be submitted to
the emperor, the eunuchs had a double check and could again
make changes to suit themselves. In addition to this process,
edicts were often promulgated directly without going through
the Grand Secretariat or any of the ministries. This meant
that in many periods edicts were in fact coming directly
from the most powerful eunuch.[40]

So-called "palace edicts" (chung-chih 中旨)--rescripts emanating from
eunuchs without regular processing through the Grand Secretariat--were
vehemently protested by the officialdom as eunuch usurpations of imperial authority.

Excessive eunuch influence in Ming times appeared most dramat-
ically in the careers of four notorious eunuch dictators: Wang Chen in
the 1440s, Wang Chih in the 1470s, Liu Chin in the early 1500s, and,
finally, the most powerful and most reviled eunuch of Chinese history,
Wei Chung-hsien in the 1620s. Dominating weak emperors, all four
disrupted the normal functioning of government as they pleased, honored
and enriched sycophantic opportunists and cruelly punished opponents,
and in general made a mockery of prescribed governmental procedures.
These were, of course, abnormal cases. The norm, from about the
1430s on, was an embarrassing but necessary collaboration between
officials and eunuchs at all levels and especially between senior grand
secretaries and eunuch leaders--a collaboration that was not without
mutual respectfulness and much of the time was marked by a sincere
intent on both sides to keep government functioning effectively. Even
so, the arrogance and recurring abusiveness of eunuchs created conditions of service that were always humiliating to Ming officials and
that subverted the traditional ruler-minister relationship.

Imperial Power: Its Limits and Effects

The structure and style of government that T'ai-tsu bequeathed to
his successors rooted power securely and unchallengeably in the throne.
It required that the emperor be actively in charge and did not permit

the emergence of any power center independent of the emperor. Moreover, it inclined emperors toward capricious and ruthless exercise of
their authority over the officialdom.

Ch'eng-tsu (1402-1424) was on the whole less capricious than his
father and, though on occasion very harsh, was attentive to his responsibilities. Jen-tsung (1424-1425), Hsüan-tsung (1425-1435), Hsiao-
tsung (1487-1505), and even the ill-fated last Ming ruler Chuang-lieh-ti
(1627-1644), though not all gentle men by any means, were conscientious
and responsive. But most other Ming rulers were inattentive. Hsien-
tsung (1464-1487) stuttered so miserably that he was ashamed to appear
at court audiences and avoided contact with his officials whenever possible. Wu-tsung (1505-1521) was a frustrated adventurer. He loved
gaiety and sport, and he often wandered about the capital in disguise,
seeking thrills in the company of sycophants. Military adventures
pleased him especially; he staged special campaigns for no purpose
other than to give himself the thrill of field leadership. In consequence
of fancied victories, he then conferred upon himself ever more distinguished military titles. Shih-tsung (1521-1566) supported a retinue of
Taoist alchemists in a prolonged search for an elixir of immortality
and for twenty years withdrew almost entirely from governmental cares,
leaving all decisions to an unpopular grand secretary. Shen-tsung (1572-
1620) was even more inattentive--so much so that modern students,
trying to peer through the veils of traditional historiography that shroud
emperors' personal lives, have speculated that he suffered glandular
disorders that made him grossly obese, or that he might have been an
opium addict. For twenty-five years he conducted no general audiences
at all, and he once went for ten years without even consulting in person
with a grand secretary. One grand secretary, finally meeting the
emperor for the first time, became so agitated that he emptied his
bladder on the palace floor and fell into a coma that lasted for several
days. What was most disruptive of all was that Shen-tsung, petulantly
determined not to be harassed by the officialdom, pigeon-holed memo-
rials in the palace and refused to make decisions even on appointments,
so that large numbers of offices fell permanently vacant and much
governmental business could not be carried on at all. Hsi-tsung (1620-
1627) refused to let governmental duties interfere with his principal
hobby, carpentry, and gave free rein to his eunuch favorite, Wei
Chung-hsien.[41]

It was under such emperors that grand secretaries or palace
eunuchs, or coalitions of both, had little choice but to exceed their
prescribed functions in order to keep the government operating, even

though it was inevitable that they would eventually be denounced as usurpers of imperial authority. It is for this reason that Chinese critics of the institutional tradition, from Huang Tsung-hsi of the seventeenth century to the present century's Ch'ien Mu, have concluded that the abolition of the Secretariat in 1380 was a climactic misfortune in the evolution of the Ming government.[42] With the disappearance of the traditional chief councilorship or prime ministership, there was no one who could legitimately wield power when the emperor neglected his duty or effectively check imperial waywardness.

Without institutional arrangements that counterbalanced emperors' powers, conscientious ministers could rely only on persuasive remonstrance to check emperors' abusiveness. Forthright remonstrance had been a significant part of the governmental heritage since antiquity. The right of every citizen to submit a written remonstrance directly to the palace was guaranteed in the Ming law code, and remonstrance functions were explicitly assigned to the censorial officials. Nevertheless, Ming government was especially ill-suited to forthright remonstrance. T'ai-tsu set the style, not only by his institutional arrangements, but by his cruel treatment of officials who opposed him. Although he officially espoused, and no doubt sincerely honored, the Confucian tradition as a whole, he was infuriated by Mencius, Confucius' most antiauthoritarian ancient interpreter. T'ai-tsu thought Mencius was disrespectful to rulers, and he said that if Mencius were still alive he would have to be punished severely. In 1394 he created a special board of scholars to edit the text of Mencius' writings, purging those passages that spoke disparagingly of the position of rulers and those that urged ministers to remonstrate against rulers' errors. In all, eighty-five passages were struck out. The emasculated edition that resulted was printed and circulated for official use in all schools.[43]

T'ai-tsu and all other Ming emperors recurringly mouthed the traditional phrases that enjoined officials to speak their minds freely. But the Ming emperors were characteristically intolerant of criticism; and the codified regulations as well as the successive imperial exhortations of the Ming period, while showing the greatest care for systematic and effective censorial surveillance over the officialdom, give little evidence that censorial or other officials were seriously encouraged to engage in remonstrance at all.

Many officials nevertheless withstood emperors to their faces in the best traditional manner. The Ming dynasty, as a matter of fact, had a disproportionately large number of China's most famous remonstrators, since Ming remonstrators were so likely to be martyred. The fifteenth-century censor Li Shih-mien 李時勉 survived after rebuking Jen-tsung for consorting with concubines during the prescribed period of mourning for his father.[44] The early sixteenth-century censor Chang Ch'in 張芹 was spared when, by bolting a frontier gate and guarding it with a sword brandished before the emperor's astonished outriders, he prevented Wu-tsung and all his entourage from touring beyond the Great Wall.[45] A junior official of the Ministry of Revenue named Hai Jui 海瑞, the interpretation of whose career became a point of great contention in mainland China's Cultural Revolution of the 1960s, remonstrated against Shih-tsung's neglect of government business and dedication to Taoist practices in 1566 and survived. On reading Hai Jui's memorial Shih-tsung flew into a rage and demanded that he not be allowed to escape. Eunuch attendants reported that Hai Jui had already said farewell to his family, had brought his coffin with him to court, and was patiently awaiting execution; then Shih-tsung relented. Nevertheless, the historical record in general is a sad one for Ming remonstrators. In 1519, when a mass of officials demonstrated against one of Wu-tsung's wasteful military outings, at least 33 men were imprisoned, 107 were forced to prostrate themselves in ranks outside the palace gate for five days, and 146 men were subjected to floggings in open court, of which 11 died. For protesting against Shih-tsung's decision in a famous ritual controversy of the 1520s, 134 remonstrators were imprisoned, numerous others were flogged in open court, some were dismissed from service, and others were exiled to frontier guard duty as common soldiers. At least 19 men are reported to have died of their punishments.[47] Shen-tsung dismissed civil servants by the dozens for remonstrating with him. In the 1620s, Hsi-tsung blacklisted more than 700 officials who were opposed to his favoring Wei Chung-hsien, and many of these suffered cruel deaths.[48]

Lo Jung-pang has protested vehemently against overemphasizing these aspects of Ming government:

> . . . To be sure, there were monarchs who concentrated
> all decision-making powers in themselves and by the force
> of their personalities were able to overawe their ministers.
> But to write about these instances as though they were the
> norm conjures up in the mind of casual readers a fantasm
> of a government by ukase; of potentates who could plunge
> the empire into war on a whim; of obsequious, groveling
> functionaries who carried out their masters' commands
> without question; and of a people cowering under the knout

and milked by corrupt officials. This is a warped picture,
a caricature, no less, of China's political institutions of
the past.[49]

His admonition is well grounded. Ming emperors could not rule single-
handedly, and once the empire had been stabilized they could not escape
the inhibiting influence of both the inherited institutions and the inherited
ideology. They as well as their officials were captives of the system.
Although neither institutional nor ideological controls could effectively
restrain an emperor from doing almost any particular thing if he were
fanatically determined to do it, the ideology largely determined what
his governmental program must be and the institutional arrangement in
practice limited the realm and effects of his capriciousness.

The gulf that T'ai-tsu had created between rulers and ministers,
by making every official's power and prestige dependent upon imperial
favor, increasingly riveted bureaucratic attention on court politics,
the realm in which imperial caprice was most operative. Favoritism
in appointments, wasteful palace expenditures, ritualistic minutiae,
the conduct of the imperial family--these became the matters over
which officials and emperors wrangled. In the larger realms of
national defense, social stability, and economic prosperity, there was
relatively little opportunity for imperial caprice, and there were few
basic disagreements between officials and emperors. Administration
in these realms therefore fell into routines that became increasingly
sacrosanct and unchallengeable. Conscientious officials went about
their routine business despite their occasional abusive treatment and
the constant possibility of it; and indolent or venal officials were unable
to immobilize or corrupt the whole governmental apparatus. From the
point of view of the people at large, to whom in the aphorism "Heaven
was high and the emperor far away," Ming government must have seemed,
on balance, stable and effective; and the nation went on its evolving way
rather comfortably for two and a half centuries without any agonizing
upheavals. Indeed, Ming Chinese might well have thought they could
not realistically conceive of a more satisfactory system. And when
the Manchus took power in 1644, they came, and were accepted, as
preservers of the system, not its challengers.

NOTES

1. F. W. Mote, The Poet Kao Ch'i (Princeton: Princeton University Press, 1962), p. 8.

2. Wu Han, Chu Yüan-chang chuan [Biography of Chu Yüan-chang] (Shanghai, 1949), pp. 66-7, translated loosely into colloquial Chinese from T'ai-tsu shih-lu (Veritable records of T'ai-tsu's reign; 1940 reprint ed.), 4: 2.

3. Wu Han, Chu Yüan-chang chuan, pp. 71-2.

4. Henry Serruys, "The Mongols in China during the Hung-wu Period (1368-1398)," Mélanges Chinois et Bouddhique, 11 (1956-59): 1-328.

5. Wu Han, Chu Yüan-chang chuan, especially pp. 101-02, 116-17, 133ff.

6. Romeyn Taylor, "The Basic Annals of Ming T'ai-tsu" (unpublished manuscript, 1970), introduction.

7. Henry Serruys, "The Mongols in China during the Hung-wu Period," pp. 42-3.

8. Romeyn Taylor, "Yüan Origins of the Wei-so System," in Chinese Government in Ming Times: Seven Studies, ed. Charles O. Hucker (New York: Columbia University Press, 1969), pp. 23-40.

9. F. W. Mote, "The Transformation of Nanking, 1350-1400" (unpublished manuscript, 1969); Edward L. Farmer, "The Dual Capital System of the Early Ming Dynasty" (Ph.D. dissertation, Harvard University, 1968).

10. Charles O. Hucker, "Governmental Organizations of the Ming Dynasty," Harvard Journal of Asiatic Studies, 21 (1958): 28.

11. Wu Han, Chu Yüan-chang chuan, especially pp. 173-75.

12. Ch'ien Mu, Kuo-shih ta-kang [Essentials of National History], 2 vols. (Taipei, 1952), 2: 481.

13. Romeyn Taylor, "Social Origins of the Ming Dynasty, 1351-1360," Monumenta Serica, 22 (1963): 60.

14. Romeyn Taylor, "Social Origins," p. 24.

15. Ku Ying-t'ai, Ming-shih chi-shih pen-mo (Ming History Arranged Topically; Kuo-hsüeh chi-pen ts'ung-shu chien-pien ed., 12 vols. in 4), II, 76 (chüan 14).

16. Ming-shih [Official History of Ming], Po-na ed. (1937), 113.1.

17. Ting I, Ming-tai t'e-wu cheng-chih [Secret-police Government in Ming times] (Peking, 1950); Robert B. Crawford, "Eunuch Power in the Ming Dynasty," T'oung Pao, vol. 49, no. 3 (1961): 115-48.

18. This discussion is taken almost verbatim from Charles O. Hucker, The Traditional Chinese State in Ming Times (Tucson: University of Arizona Press, 1961), pp. 25-7.

19. Ray Huang, "Fiscal Administration during the Ming Dynasty," in Chinese Government in Ming Times, ed. Charles O. Hucker, pp. 73-128, especially pp. 125-28.

20. This discussion is taken almost verbatim from Charles O. Hucker, The Traditional Chinese State, pp. 30-1.

21. Hoshi Ayao, The Ming Tribute Grain System, trans. Mark Elvin (Ann Arbor, Michigan: Center for Chinese Studies, 1969), p. 8.

22. Lo Jung-pang, "Policy Formulation and Decision-Making on Issues Respecting Peace and War," in Chinese Government in Ming Times, ed. Charles O. Hucker, pp. 41-72; the citation is from p. 51.

23. Lo Jung-pang, "Policy Formulation," pp. 52-3.

24. F. W. Mote, The Poet Kao Ch'i, p. 36; and F. W. Mote, "The Growth of Chinese Despotism," Oriens Extremus, 8 (1961): 1-41. Cf. Li Kuang-pi, Ming-ch'ao shih-lüeh [Brief History of the Ming Dynasty] (Wuhan, 1957); Wu Han, Chu Yüan-chang chuan; and S. Y. Teng, "Ming T'ai-tsu's Destructive and Constructive Work," Chinese Culture, 8 (1967): 14-38; passim.

25. Wu Han, Chu Yüan-chang chuan, especially pp. 101-02, 133-44.

26. Frank Münzel, "Some Remarks on Ming T'ai-tsu" (unpublished manuscript, 1968).

27. F. W. Mote, "The Growth of Chinese Despotism," p. 28.

28. Ch'ien Mu, Kuo-shih ta-kang, 2: 476-77, citing Ts'ao-mu-tzu (miscellanea by Yeh Tzu-ch'i).

29. F. W. Mote, "The Growth of Chinese Despotism," p. 34. One comma has been added.

30. See Hoshi Ayao, The Ming Tribute Grain System; Wu Chi-hua, Ming-tai hai-yün chi yün-ho ti yen-chiu [A Study on Transportation by Sea and the Grand Canal in the Ming Dynasty] (Taipei, 1961); and Ray Huang, "The Grand Canal during the Ming Dynasty" (Ph.D. dissertation, University of Michigan, 1964).

31. See Henry Serruys, Sino-Jurced Relations during the Yung-lo Period (Wiesbaden: Otto Harrassowitz, 1955); Li Chi, "Manchuria in History," Chinese Social and Political Science Review, 16 (1932-33): 226-59; and T. C. Lin, "Manchuria in the Ming Empire," Nankai Social and Economic Quarterly, 8 (1935): 1-43.

32. Wang Yi-t'ung, Official Relations between China and Japan, 1368-1549 (Cambridge, Mass.: Harvard University Press, 1953), pp. 10-59.

33. J. J. L. Duyvendak, China's Discovery of Africa (London: Arthur Probsthain, 1949); Paul Pelliot, "Les Grands Voyages Maritimes Chinois au Début XVe Siècle," T'oung Pao, 30 (1933): 237-452; and J. J. L. Duyvendak, "The True Dates of the Chinese Maritime Expeditions in the Early Fifteenth Century," T'oung Pao, 34 (1938): 341-412.

34. Lo Jung-pang, "The Decline of the Early Ming Navy," Oriens Extremus, 5 (1958): 149-68.

35. This discussion is taken almost verbatim from Charles O. Hucker, "Governmental Organization," pp. 39-42.

36. Tilemann Grimm, "Das Neiko der Ming-Zeit von den Anfängen bis 1506," Oriens Extremus, 1 (1954): 139-77.

37. Much of the foregoing discussion duplicates Charles O. Hucker, "Governmental Organization," pp. 29-31.

38. Ting I, Ming-tai t'e-wu cheng-chih.

39. U. H. Mammitzsch, "Wei Chung-hsien (1568-1628): a Reappraisal of the Eunuch and the Factional Strife at the Late Ming Court" (Ph.D. dissertation, University of Hawaii, 1968), pp. 30-1.

40. Robert B. Crawford, "Eunuch Power," p. 135. The word "period" in the original has been changed to "periods."

41. This discussion is taken almost verbatim from Charles O. Hucker, The Censorial System of Ming China (Stanford: Stanford University Press, 1966), pp. 42-3.

42. Wm. T. de Bary, "Chinese Despotism and the Chinese Ideal: a Seventeenth-century View," in Chinese Thought and Institutions, ed. John K. Fairbank (Chicago: University of Chicago Press, 1957), p. 175; Ch'ien Mu, Chung-kuo li-tai cheng-chih te-shih [Critique of Governance in Chinese History] (Hong Kong, 1952), pp. 79-85.

43. Wu Han, Chu Yüan-chang chuan, pp. 148-49.

44. Charles O. Hucker, The Censorial System, pp. 113-15.

45. Wolfgang Seuberlich, "Kaisertrue oder Auflehnung? Eine Episode aus der Ming-Zeit," Zeitschrift der Deutschen Morgenländischen Gesellschaft, vol. 102 (1952): 304-14.

46. Hsia Hsieh, Ming t'ung-chien [Chronological History of Ming] (Peking, 1959) 4 vols., pp. 2473-75 (chüan 63); cf. James R. Pusey, Wu Han: Attacking the Present through the Past (Cambrdige, Mass.: Harvard University Press, 1969).

47. Charles O. Hucker, "Confucianism and the Chinese Censorial System," in Confucianism in Action, ed. David S. Nivison and Arthur F. Wright (Stanford: Stanford University Press, 1959), pp. 200-01.

48. Charles O. Hucker, "The Tung-lin Movement of the Late Ming Period," in Chinese Thought and Institutions, ed. John K. Fairbank, pp. 153ff.

49. Lo Jung-pang, "Policy Formulation," p. 43.

MICHIGAN PAPERS IN CHINESE STUDIES

No. 2. The Cultural Revolution: 1967 in Review, four essays by Michel Oksenberg, Carl Riskin, Robert Scalapino, and Ezra Vogel.

No. 3. Two Studies in Chinese Literature, by Li Chi and Dale Johnson.

No. 4. Early Communist China: Two Studies, by Ronald Suleski and Daniel Bays.

No. 5. The Chinese Economy, ca. 1870-1911, by Albert Feuerwerker.

No. 6. Chinese Paintings in Chinese Publications, 1956-1968: An Annotated Bibliography and an Index to the Paintings, by E. J. Laing.

No. 7. The Treaty Ports and China's Modernization: What Went Wrong? by Rhoads Murphey.

No. 8. Two Twelfth Century Texts on Chinese Painting, by Robert J. Maeda.

No. 9. The Economy of Communist China, 1949-1969, by Chu-yuan Cheng.

No. 10. Educated Youth and the Cultural Revolution in China, by Martin Singer.

No. 11. Premodern China: A Bibliographical Introduction, by Chun-shu Chang.

No. 12. Two Studies on Ming History, by Charles O. Hucker.

No. 13. Nineteenth Century China: Five Imperialist Perspectives, selected by Dilip Basu, edited by Rhoads Murphey.

No. 14. Modern China, 1840-1972: An Introduction to Sources and Research Aids, by Andrew J. Nathan.

No. 15. Women in China: Studies in Social Change and Feminism, edited by Marilyn B. Young.

No. 16. An Annotated Bibliography of Chinese Painting Catalogues and Related Texts, by Hin-cheung Lovell.

No. 17. China's Allocation of Fixed Capital Investment, 1952-1957, by Chu-yuan Cheng.

No. 18. Health, Conflict, and the Chinese Political System, by David M. Lampton.

No. 19. Chinese and Japanese Music-Dramas, edited by J. I. Crump and William P. Malm.

MICHIGAN ABSTRACTS OF CHINESE AND
JAPANESE WORKS ON CHINESE HISTORY

No. 1. The Ming Tribute Grain System, by Hoshi Ayao, translated by Mark Elvin.

No. 2. Commerce and Society in Sung China, by Shiba Yoshinobu, translated by Mark Elvin.

No. 3. Transport in Transition: The Evolution of Traditional Shipping in China, translations by Andrew Watson.

No. 4. Japanese Perspectives on China's Early Modernization: A Bibliographical Survey, by K. H. Kim.

No. 5. The Silk Industry in Ch'ing China, by Shih Min-hsiung, translated by E-tu Zen Sun.

NONSERIES PUBLICATION

Index to the "Chan-kuo Ts'e," by Sharon Fidler and J. I. Crump. A companion volume to the Chan-kuo Ts'e, translated by J. I. Crump (Oxford: Clarendon Press, 1970).

Michigan Papers and Abstracts available from:

Center for Chinese Studies
The University of Michigan
Lane Hall (Publications)
Ann Arbor, MI 48109 USA

Prepaid Orders Only
write for complete price listing

Printed and bound by CPI Group (UK) Ltd, Croydon, CR0 4YY

13/04/2025

14656536-0005